Meet the Miniature Schnauzer

- The Miniature Schnauzer is classified as being a member of the Terrier group of dogs.

- Miniature Schnauzers were originally bred to be stable or farm dogs; used as ratters and guard dogs.

- Germany is the Miniature Schnauzer's country of origin.

- The name schnauzer (pronounced SHNOW-rsa in German) means snout, muzzle, spout or nose, which is a suitable name for this sniffing dog.

- The Miniature Schnauzer is available in three coat varieties: salt and pepper, solid black, black and silver.

- When it comes to grooming, the Miniature Schnauzer is a high-maintenance dog, whose double coat needs professional attention every few months.

- The versatile Miniature Schnauzer has a full supply of energy, and enjoys plenty of exercise.

- Miniature Schnauzers make sturdy playmates for kids and are excellent watchdogs, too!

- Generally, the Miniature Schnauzer enjoys training sessions and is a quick learner.

- The Miniature Schnauzer is described as being devoted and playful. He is a sweet, proud dog who loves to be the center of the household.

Featuring Photographs by
JEANNIE AND BANE HARRISON OF CLOSE ENCOUNTERS OF
THE FURRY KIND

Howell Book House
Published by Wiley Publishing, Inc. All rights reserved
Published simultaneously in Canada

Limit of Liability/Disclaimer of Warranty: While the publisher and the author
have used their best efforts in preparing this book, they make no representa-
tions or warranties with respect to the accuracy or completeness of the contents
of this book and specifically disclaim any implied warranties of merchantability
or fitness for a particular purpose. No warranty may be created or extended by
sales representatives or written sales materials. The advice and strategies con-
tained herein may not be suitable for your situation. You should consult with a
professional where appropriate. Neither the publisher nor the author shall be
liable for any loss of profit or any other commercial damages, including but not
limited to special, incidental, consequential, or other damages.

For general information about our other products and services, please contact
our Customer Care Department within the United States at (800) 762-2974,
outside the United States at (317) 572-3993 or fax (317) 572-4002.

Wiley also publishes its books in a variety of electronic formats. Some content
that appears in print may not be available in electronic books. For more information about Wiley products, visit our web site at www.wiley.com.

The Essential Miniature Schnauzer is an abridged edition of *The Miniature
Schnauzer: An Owner's Guide to a Happy Healthy Pet*, first published in 1996.

Library of Congress Cataloging-in-Publication Data
The essential miniature schnauzer / featuring photographs by Jeannie and
Bane Harrison.
   p. cm.   Includes bibliographical references
   ISBN 1-58245-069-2
   1. Miniature Schnauzer.
SF429.M58E77   1999   99-10094
636.755—dc21   CIP

Manufactured in the United States of America
10 9 8 7 6 5

Series Director: Michele Matrisciani
Production Team: David Faust, Heather Pope, and Carol Sheehan
Book Design: Paul Costello

ARE YOU READY?!

☐ Have you prepared your home and your family for your new pet?

☐ Have you gotten the proper supplies you'll need to care for your dog?

☐ Have you found a veterinarian that you (and your dog) are comfortable with?

☐ Have you thought about how you want your dog to behave?

☐ Have you arranged your schedule to accommodate your dog's needs for exercise and attention?

No matter what stage you're at with your dog—still thinking about getting one, or he's already part of the family—this Essential guide will provide you with the practical information you need to understand and care for your canine companion. Of course you're ready—you have this book!

THE ESSENTIAL

Miniature Schnauzer

The Miniature Schnauzer's Senses

SIGHT

Miniature Schnauzers can detect movement at a greater distance than we can, but they can't see as well up close. They can also see better in less light, but can't distinguish many colors.

SOUND

Miniature Schnauzers, like all dogs, can hear about four times better than we can, and they can hear high-pitched sounds especially well.

TASTE

Miniature Schnauzers have fewer taste buds than we do, so they're likelier to try anything—and usually do, which is why it's important for their owners to monitor their food intake. Dogs are omnivorous, which means they eat meat as well as vegetables.

TOUCH

Miniature Schnauzers are social animals and love to be petted, groomed and played with.

SMELL

The Miniature Schnauzer is a serious sniffer, so his nose is his greatest sensory organ! A dog's sense of smell is so great he can follow a trail that's weeks old, detect odors diluted to one-millionth the concentration we'd need to notice them, even sniff out a person under water!

CHAPTER ONE

Getting to Know Your Miniature Schnauzer

In essence, the Miniature Schnauzer knows he can get by with just about anything because he's amusing, smart, tough, eye–catching, clever and knows how to handle you. He is convinced he's the best thing that ever happened to you and knows you're the best thing that ever happened to him. He is, after all, a Miniature Schnauzer. And you are, after all, his best friend, house-keeper, chef, caretaker and landlord. How lucky can you be? In return, he loves you and responds to your every wish—when he's in the mood. A fair exchange, he figures.

Your Miniature Schnauzer enjoys life because he can find his own amusement. He's smart and he knows it. He's tough enough and he knows it (though we know he's not as tough as he thinks). He knows he's a knockout traffic stopper, and

This Miniature Schnauzer knows how to have fun all on his own!

he takes pleasure in cleverly out-smarting you. He recognizes your mood and knows when outsmarting you will make you laugh and when it'll get him into trouble.

AN EXCELLENT ALARM DOG

To his credit, the Miniature Schnauzer considers salesmen, deliv-ery services and unknown visitors as intruders—a view that should be respected. It makes no sense to end his value as a watchdog. What does make sense is for him to learn that his alarming barks should cease at your, not his, discretion; you're only

training him when to stop an alarm or warning bark, not to eliminate it or its value.

When you've reached the final phase of training to time the dog's dutiful alarm barking and minimize the decibel factor of his normal day-to-day barking, you'll think you have it made. Wrong! There is one con-cession you must make to overcome a Miniature Schnauzer's intrinsic need to vocalize and exhibit stub-bornness. He will have the last word. His life depends on it. Without it, he won't get through the next five minutes. In spite of your dedicated training, in spite of his dedication to you, he will have one last grunt.

A SERIOUS SNIFFER

His instinct as a ratter makes him a natural for serious sniffing. His curious nature is credible, but a sniffing habit becomes an annoyance during a simple walk down the street.

A DAY IN THE LIFE OF A MINIATURE SCHNAUZER

With his barking and sniffing instincts narrowed to an acceptable measure, the Miniature Schnauzer becomes a dog of considerable versatility. He enjoys a comfortable lap with the same quiet satisfaction as does any toy breed (all of whom are bred for lap-sitting duty).

Most Miniature Schnauzers will enjoy dress-up time, as they're decked out in fake antlers at Christmas, a frilly Easter bonnet, Halloween ghost garb or in a tuxedo, tutu or clown suit. Those who do consider the costuming a demeaning frivolity manage to endure the embarrassment without much glee but with small objection.

As a non-shedding breed, many Miniature Schnauzers are allowed (if not welcomed) to enjoy the comfort

CHARACTERISTICS OF THE MINIATURE SCHNAUZER

Smart	Curious
Likes to bark	Fun-loving
Stubborn at times	Agreeable
Doesn't shed	Very trainable

of chairs, sofas and beds. He'll happily cuddle next to you if you're napping or bedded down for the night. If you awaken to a more distantly positioned dog, he didn't tire of your companionship; he moved to cooler comfort.

If your preference is to strictly forbid all comfort from chair, sofa and bed, expect obedience from the

3

This little guy can't fight his instinct to sniff.

Owners don't mind when their Miniature Schnauzers veg out on the sofa—there's no loose hair left behind!

4

dog in your presence, but don't bet on his compliance in your absence. Good odds are that he'll leap to the floor from the no-no at the sound of your return. That move to comfort isn't misbehavior, it's a sign of intelligence, as is his hiding the evidence.

PLAYTIME!

With his costumes, lap-sitting, cuddling, naps and meals out of the way, it's playtime, a Miniature Schnauzer–required activity. Armed with a toy, he'll amuse himself

endlessly. If he's toyless, he'll manufacture a game. A moving shadow on the floor (as tree limbs sway outside on a breezy day) offers paw-pouncing challenges; a housefly elicits a superb degree of eye-darting and air-chomping; the click of temperature-changing appliances (the refrigerator, furnace or air conditioner) requires his attentive watchfulness for the next click—he dares it to fail. Very few natural or man-made noises, movements or objects are incapable of his play-creation efforts.

It is a wonder, with his innate curiosity and busy attitude, that the Miniature Schnauzer is not hyperactive. He has managed to be intensely curious, busy, playful and fun-loving, with a nicely balanced acceptance and need for quiet times and activities. He reaches an extremely agreeable happy medium. Children must learn not to tax that happy medium by overexhausting him.

AN EAGER LEARNER

This is a dog that really likes to learn. After one class session (whether it's puppy, obedience, conformation, agility, etc.), he'll look forward to the next, if only because he's such a quick learner. While being trained to execute any part of an exercise that typically elicits an aggressive response from many terrier breeds, any objection the Miniature Schnauzer may have won't be physical; it'll merely be a refusal, but he will eventually get around to the exercise. The Miniature Schnauzer is very trainable. Expect a snag or regression—every dog experiences the phenomenon—but your perky little learner will bounce back, recovering nicely.

The "TTT" (Typical Terrible Terrier) syndrome doesn't apply to our Miniature Schnauzer. He's untypically agreeable.

5

CHAPTER TWO

Homecoming

What an exciting time! A puppy is entering your life, and even more exciting—she's a Miniature Schnauzer, who'll grab your heart as you grab hers. Aware of the responsibility that accompanies her, you're prepared, long before her arrival, with all of her needs. Since her first two weeks in your home will be highly stressful for her

(and you), your preparedness will minimize her anxiety and heighten your joyful anticipation.

PUT TO THE TEST

Choosing a puppy is usually a happy expedition to a breeder's home or kennel. Do not be put off if your puppy's owner puts you through the third degree, asking questions like, "Where will the puppy sleep? Where will the puppy stay while you're at work? Do you have a fenced-in yard? If you owned a dog before, what happened to her?" All of these questions are designed to determine whether yours is a suitable home for the sweet puppy.

PICKING YOUR PUPPY

We shall assume you pass the "test" easily. Now, which puppy in the litter will be yours? The breeder may offer you a choice of only one or two. That's perfectly all right. There are very likely to be reservations for one or more of the babies— people who left deposits even before birth. Excellent breeders are sometimes booked well in advance of whelping.

If you do have a choice, be sure to pick a lively, alert animal, one who bounces up to greet you and wants to interact with the family. Do not be taken by the shy, shivering pup in the corner, no matter how sorry you may feel for her.

Before bringing home your new family member, do a little planning to help make the transition easier. The first decision to make is where the puppy will live. Will she have access to the entire house or be limited to certain rooms? A similar consideration applies to the yard. It is simpler to control a puppy's activities and to housetrain the puppy if

This pillow has been a favorite of this Miniature Schnauzer since she was a pup.

Miniature Schnauzer puppies need human companionship and shouldn't be left alone for long periods of time.

she is confined to definite areas. If doors do not exist where needed, baby gates make satisfactory temporary barriers.

One of the most important things to take care of before you bring your new Miniature Schnauzer home is selecting a veterinarian to whose care you'll entrust your puppy. You can rely on the recommendations of dog-owning friends and neighbors, or other knowledgeable sources. After your puppy's arrival (preferably within forty-eight hours), your veterinarian should give her a checkup

A dog crate will provide your Miniature Schnauzer with a safe place to rest or play.

and vaccination schedule, and answer any questions you may have.

A dog crate is an excellent investment and is an invaluable aid in raising a puppy. It provides a safe, quiet place where a dog can sleep. If it's used properly, a crate helps with housetraining. However, long periods of uninterrupted stays are not recommended—especially for young puppies. Unless you have someone at home or can have someone come in a few times a day to let her out to relieve herself and socialize with her for a while, a small crate is not advisable. Never lock a young puppy in a small crate for more than one hour without giving her an opportunity to relieve herself.

Make sure your Miniature Schnauzer will have company and companionship during the day. If the members of your family are not at home during the day, try to come home at lunchtime, let your puppy out and spend some time with her. If this isn't possible, try to get a neighbor or friend who lives close by to come spend time with the puppy. Your Miniature Schnauzer thrives on human attention and guidance, and a puppy left alone most of the day will find ways to get your attention, most of them not

PUPPY ESSENTIALS

To prepare yourself and your family for your puppy's homecoming, and to be sure your pup has what she needs, you should obtain the following:

Food and Water Bowls: One for each. We recommend stainless steel or heavy crockery—something solid but easy to clean.

Bed and/or Crate Pad: Something soft, washable and big enough for your soon-to-be-adult dog.

Crate: Make housetraining easier and provide a safe, secure den for your dog with a crate—it only looks like a cage to you!

Toys: As much fun to buy as they are for your pup to play with. Don't overwhelm your puppy with too many toys, though, especially the first few days she's home. And be sure to include something hollow you can stuff with goodies, like a Kong.

I.D. Tag: Inscribed with your name and phone number.

Collar: An adjustable buckle collar is best. Remember, your pup's going to grow fast!

Leash: Style is nice, but durability and your comfort while holding it count, too. You can't go wrong with leather for most dogs.

Grooming Supplies: The proper brushes, special shampoo, toenail clippers, a toothbrush and doggy toothpaste.

After a long day at play, this pup takes a well-deserved nap.

so cute and many downright destructive.

ACCESSORIES

The breeder should tell you what your puppy has been eating. Buy some of this food and have it on hand when your puppy arrives. Keep the puppy on the food and feeding schedule of the breeder, especially for the first few days. If you want to switch foods after that, introduce the new one slowly, gradually adding more and more to the old until it has been entirely replaced.

Your puppy will need a close-fitting nylon or cotton-webbed collar. This collar should be adjustable so that it can be used for the first couple of months. A properly fit collar is tight enough that it will not slip over the head, yet an adult finger fits easily under it. A puppy should never wear a choke chain or any other adult training collar.

In addition to a collar, you'll need a 4-to-6-foot-long leash. One made of nylon or cotton-webbed material is a fine and inexpensive first leash. It does not need to be more than half an inch in width. It is important to make sure that the clip is of excellent quality and cannot become unclasped on its own. You will need one or two leads for walking the dog, as well as a collar or harness. If you live in a cold climate, a sweater or jacket for excursions with your Miniature Schnauzer would be appropriate. Get a somewhat larger size than you immediately need to allow for growth.

Excessive chewing can be partially resolved by providing a puppy with her own chew toys. Small-size dog biscuits are good for the teeth and also act as an amusing toy. Do not buy chew toys composed of compressed particles, as these particles disintegrate when chewed and can get stuck in the puppy's throat. Hard rubber toys are also good for chewing, as are large rawhide bones. Avoid the smaller chewsticks, as they can splinter and choke the puppy. Anything given to a dog must be large enough that it cannot be swallowed.

The final starter items a puppy will need are a water bowl and food dish. You can select a smaller food dish for your puppy and then get a bigger one when your dog matures. Bowls are available in plastic, stainless steel and even ceramic. Stainless steel is probably the best choice, as it is practically indestructible. Nonspill dishes are available for the dog that likes to play in her water.

Identification

You will have to provide your puppy with some means of identification. The first option is a common identification tag attached to the puppy's collar, bearing your name and phone number. This is the first thing someone who finds your Miniature Schnauzer will look for, and the information on it is straightforward and accessible. However, puppies can easily slip out of collars, and tags can fall off, so it is important to have a more permanent method of identification as well.

It is important to provide your pet with an adjustable collar and identification tag.

IDENTIFY YOUR DOG

It is a terrible thing to think about, but your dog could somehow, someday, get lost or stolen. For safety's sake, every dog should wear a buckle collar with an identification tag. A tag is the first thing a stranger will look for on a lost dog. Inscribe the tag with your dog's name and your name and phone number.

There are two ways to permanently identify your dog. The first is a tattoo, placed on the inside of your dog's thigh. The tattoo should be your Social Security number or your dog's AKC registration number. The second is a microchip, a rice-sized pellet that is inserted under the dog's skin at the base of the neck, between the shoulder blades. When a scanner is passed over the dog, it will beep, notifying the person that the dog has a chip. The scanner will then show a code, identifying the dog.

A microchip can also be used to identify your dog. A veterinarian can inject a tiny microchip encoded with your Miniature Schnauzer's information under her skin. Many animal shelters and vet's offices have the scanner to read the chip, and it cannot get lost or be removed. However, until the scanners (expensive pieces of equipment) are more widely available, it is preferable to choose another form of identification as well.

The third method is a tattoo of some identifying number (your Social Security number, or your dog's AKC number) placed on the inside of your dog's hind leg. A tattoo is easily noticed and located, and it requires no sophisticated machinery to read. Anyone finding a lost dog with a tattoo will inform a vet or local animal shelter who will know what to do.

The single best preventive measure one can take to ensure that a dog is not lost or stolen is to house-train and chew-toy train your Miniature Schnauzer so she may safely and comfortably spend her days indoors. If your dog is an indoor/outdoor dog, a completely fenced yard is a must. If you have a fence, it should be carefully inspected to insure there are no holes or gaps in it, and no places where a vigorous and mischievous puppy could escape by digging an escape path under the fence.

PUPPY-PROOFING

Outside

If you do not have a fenced yard, it would be useful to provide at least an outside kennel area where the puppy could safely relieve herself. Failing that, but only after 3 months of age, the youngster should be walked outdoors on a lead several times a day, taking care at first that the lead is sufficiently tight around her neck so that she cannot slip out of it.

Inside

You will also need to puppy-proof your home. Curious puppies will get into everything everywhere. Even if you generally keep your Miniature Schnauzer close to you or in her indoor or outdoor enclosure, there will be times when she wants to explore and you cannot watch her. Make sure your home has been puppy-proofed so you can be reasonably confident she won't do serious damage to herself or your home.

Securely stow away all household cleaners and other poisonous products, such as antifreeze which, unfortunately, has a taste dogs seem to love. Keep all electrical cords out of reach, and secure electrical outlets.

Make sure you have removed poisonous plants from your house and garden. Puppies put everything into their mouths, and you need to

HOUSEHOLD DANGERS

Curious puppies and inquisitive dogs get into trouble not because they are bad, but simply because they want to investigate the world around them. It's our job to protect our dogs from harmful substances, like the following:

In the Garage

antifreeze

garden supplies, like snail and slug bait, pesticides, fertilizers, mouse and rat poisons

In the House

cleaners, especially pine oil

perfumes, colognes, aftershaves

medications, vitamins

office and craft supplies

electric cords

chicken or turkey bones

chocolate, onions

some house and garden plants, like ivy, oleander and poinsettia

make sure there's nothing dangerous they can get into. Inside, dangerous plants include poinsettia, ivy and philodendron. Outside, holly, hydrangea and azalea are among the plants of which your puppy should steer clear. The bulbs and root systems of daffodils, tulips and others are also poisonous.

THE ALL-IMPORTANT ROUTINE

Most puppies do best if their lives follow a schedule. They need definite and regular periods of time for playing, eating and sleeping. Puppies like to start their day early. This is a good time to take a walk or play some games of fetch. After breakfast, most are ready for a nap. How often this pattern is repeated will depend on one's daily routine. Sometimes it is easier for a working person or family to stick with a regular schedule than it is for someone who is home all of the time.

Most dogs reach their peaks of activity and need the least amount of rest from 6 months to 3 years of age. As they mature, they spend increasingly longer periods of time sleeping. It is important to make an effort to ensure that a Miniature Schnauzer receives sufficient exercise each day to keep her in proper weight and fitness throughout her life. Puppies need short periods of exercise, but, due to the fact that their bodies are developing, should never be exercised to excess.

14

Puppies and adult dogs need a daily routine of scheduled time for playing, exercising, eating and sleeping.

CHAPTER THREE

To Good Health

If you don't have a trusted veterinarian already, ask your breeder or other Miniature Schnauzer owners in the area for recommendations. Call veterinarians in your area and ask if they've treated Miniature Schnauzers before. Also ask what their policies are on visits, emergency care and anything else you're concerned with.

Once at the veterinarian's, pay attention to how the staff and the vet handle your dog. Is the waiting room clean and comfortable for the animals? Do you have to wait a long time with no explanation why? Is the veterinarian interested in answering your questions and does he or she handle your dog

well? If you don't get a good feeling about the people or the place, keep looking.

It's your responsibility to be a good patient, too. Train your Miniature Schnauzer to accept handling by the veterinarian. Get him used to the vet's office by taking him in every once in a while even if he doesn't have an appointment.

Many dogs get anxious in a vet's office between the smells and strange animals. They associate the place with bad things, and no wonder! It's your job to make your veterinarian's job easier by paying attention to your dog's condition and training him to be polite. These are easy things to do with a lovable Miniature Schnauzer.

FIRST THINGS FIRST

Some health problems that affect Miniature Schnauzers are the result of breeding; they are inherited conditions passed down through family lines. Because the Miniature Schnauzer is a breed that requires frequent and specialized grooming, your opportunity to detect any suspicious or superficial change is maximized.

Skin Problems

SCHNAUZER BUMPS—Many Miniature Schnauzers have small wartlike nodes on their skin; these are uniquely known as schnauzer bumps. Schnauzer bumps exude nothing, they simply exist, and typically bother the dog's owner far more than the dog; actually, he is not bothered by them at all. Much has been written about why they crop up and what to do about them, and opinions on the subject vary. Perhaps someday their mystery will be solved. Meanwhile, the logical step for a disturbed owner is to hide the bumps beneath longer hair. If you see bumps from which a fatty, oily substance is secreted, they are not just schnauzer bumps and need medication.

SEBORRHEA—This results from an alteration in the production of skin oils, causing a flaky, scaly skin or greasy, yellow-brown scales. A dog suffering from seborrhea will often have a rancid smell. Seborrhea in Miniature Schnauzers is sometimes incurable, but may be kept under control with a special shampoo.

HOT SPOTS—These are skin infections that appear as patches of red, irritated skin with hair loss. The spots seem to form overnight, and are caused by the dog constantly licking or scratching at the infected spot. Hot spots are easy to treat with Allercaine to make the dog stop licking at the spot.

Healthy skin is smooth and flexible with no visible scales, scabs, growths or red areas; is dandruff-free; is not excessively oily; and has no bald areas (except during the stages of a stripped coat, which is a special grooming technique).

To prevent your dog from worsening any skin problem by biting an itch or licking a wound, saturate a cloth with mouthwash, place it on the spot and rub it gently through the coat to reach the skin. Dogs hate the taste and the product contains nothing harmful.

Eye Problems

Eyes should be bright, shiny and free from excessive tearing or discharge. The conjunctiva (the moist, pink inner lining of the eyelids) should not be swollen, inflamed or have a yellow discharge. If any of these conditions are noted, the causes are widely varied.

This owner keeps a close eye on the condition of her Miniature Schnauzer's skin.

17

PRA (PROGRESSIVE RETINAL ATROPHY)—is a genetic (inherited) eye disease in which the cells of the retina gradually degenerate, leading to loss of sight. Initially, your dog will lose night vision, and he'll eventually go blind. PRA affects Miniature Schnauzers and many other breeds. Interestingly, however, the severity of PRA affects different breeds at different ages, causing some to lose their sight within months and others, years. While the disease itself cannot be cured, its elimination in a breed may be possible through discriminate breeding. PRA-affected dogs obviously must not be bred.

PREVENTIVE CARE PAYS

Using common sense, paying attention to your dog and working with your veterinarian, you can minimize health risks and problems. Use vet-recommended flea, tick and heartworm preventive medications; feed a nutritious diet appropriate for your dog's size, age and activity level; give your dog sufficient exercise and regular grooming; train and socialize your dog; keep current on your dog's shots; and enjoy all the years you have with your friend.

This Miniature Schnauzer is happy and healthy—you can see it in his eyes!

To determine the presence or absence of the disease in a dog, his eyes must be examined annually by a board-certified veterinary ophthalmologist, who sends the test findings to the Canine Eye Registration Foundation (CERF), located at Purdue University, where the results of each breed's eye tests are analyzed. Annual eye tests are necessary because a dog's early tests may find his eyes to be unaffected, but a later test may show the disease. Through massive and costly studies, the DNA factors that identify carriers have been discovered in the Irish Setter and Miniature Schnauzer.

PRA is expressed in a pattern unique to the Miniature Schnauzer. One form affects puppies, who lose their sight between 8 and 12 months of age. Another form affects adults, who become blind at around 3 years of age.

The American Miniature Schnauzer Club has made a strong commitment to raise $175,000 to fund a three-year study by the Baker Institute for Animal Health at Cornell University, hopefully to discover the DNA factors that determine PRA carriers in the Miniature Schnauzer—offering the potential to significantly benefit many breeds.

CATARACTS—are as common in older dogs as they are in older

humans. The lens becomes clouded by an opacity that is milky gray or bluish white in color. The degree of loss of vision varies from dog to dog, and when blindness occurs, surgical removal of the lens can restore functional vision. On the other hand, **congenital juvenile cataracts (CJC)** are genetic in nature and untreatable. Like PRA, the condition is discoverable in the dog's annual eye examinations, and affects all breeds of dogs, including the Miniature Schnauzer.

EAR PROBLEMS

Attention to the cleaning of your dog's ear canals will acquaint you with the appearance and characteristics of a normal, healthy ear, in which a slight collection of wax is normal, which has no odor and whose inside skin is light pink in color. If your dog has cropped ears, this healthy condition should be prevalent. Your Miniature Schnauzer needs veterinary care if the inside of the ear is swollen or tender, has a foul odor, has a profuse collection of wax, if a sloshing noise is heard when he shakes his head or if the inside skin color is red.

These could all be signs of an inner ear infection, probably caused by yeast, bacteria or ear mites. Yeast and bacteria grow rapidly in dark, damp areas, which is why the inner ear is an ideal spot for them. You won't be able to tell the difference between a bacterial or a yeast infection; your veterinarian will have to perform a test to see what it is. Ear mites cause a dog to scratch at his ears frequently and shake his head. They are microscopic, so it will take your veterinarian to see them. They can also cause a brown, waxy discharge. Your vet will also need to treat the ears to flush them out.

Any ear problem will worsen if untreated. If ointment or ear drops

Sneaking a peek into your dog's ear can prevent wax and dirt from turning into infections.

Your Miniature Schnauzer counts on you to keep him healthy so he can play.

are recommended, place the medication into the ear and gently massage the area just below the canal in order to channel the medication deeply into the ear's lower compartment.

You can prevent ear infections from happening by cleaning your dog's ears regularly. There are special preparations you can buy in your pet supply store that do a fine job. Follow the directions, using cotton and plastic gloves if you want. Never use cotton swabs. These can damage the eardrum if pushed in at the wrong angle.

THE IMPORTANCE OF PREVENTIVE CARE

There are many aspects of preventive care with which Miniature Schnauzer owners should be familiar: vaccinations, regular vet visits and tooth care are just some. The advantage of preventive care is that it prevents problems.

The earlier that illness is detected in the Miniature Schnauzer, the easier it is for the veterinarian to treat the problem. Owners can help ensure their dogs' health by being on the lookout for medical problems. All this requires is an eye for detail and a willingness to observe. Pay close attention to your Miniature Schnauzer, how he looks, how he acts. What is normal behavior? How does his coat usually look? What are his eating and sleeping patterns? Subtle changes can indicate a problem. Keep close tabs on what is normal for your Miniature Schnauzer, and if anything out of the ordinary develops, call the veterinarian.

Spaying and Neutering

Spaying or neutering—surgically altering the Miniature Schnauzer so she or he cannot reproduce—should be at the top of every owner's "To Do" list. Why?

First, every day thousands of puppies are born in the United States as a result of uncontrolled breeding. For every pet living in a happy home today, there are four pets on the street or in abusive homes suffering from starvation, exposure, neglect or mistreatment. In six years, a single female dog and her offspring can be the source of 67,000 new dogs.

ADVANTAGES OF SPAY/NEUTER

The greatest advantage of spaying (for females) or neutering (for males) your dog is that you are guaranteed that your dog will not produce puppies. There are too many puppies already available for too few homes. There are other advantages as well.

Advantages of Spaying

No messy heats.

No "suitors" howling at your windows or waiting in your yard.

No risk of pyometra (disease of the uterus) and decreased incidences of mammary cancer.

Advantages of Neutering

Decreased incidences of fighting, but does not affect the dog's personality.

Decreased roaming in search of bitches in season.

Decreased incidences of many urogenital diseases.

A second reason to spay or neuter your Miniature Schnauzer is to create a healthier, more well-adjusted pet that, in most cases, will live longer than an intact animal. A spayed female is less prone to the

21

YOUR PUPPY'S VACCINES

Vaccines are given to prevent your dog from getting infectious diseases like canine distemper or rabies. Vaccines are the ultimate preventive medicine: They're given before your dog ever gets the disease so as to protect him from the disease. That's why it is necessary for your dog to be vaccinated routinely. Puppy vaccines start at 8 weeks of age for the five-in-one DHLPP vaccine and are given every three to four weeks until the puppy is 16 months old. Your veterinarian will put your puppy on a proper schedule and will remind you when to bring in your dog for shots.

risk of pyometra, and uterine, ovarian and mammary cancers, and the procedure eliminates the behavior that accompanies the female's heat cycle. A neutered male is less likely to develop prostate cancer and is less apt to roam. Marking behavior is also reduced by altering. Finally, a neutered male will be picked on less by other male dogs.

When should your Miniature Schnauzer be spayed or neutered? Recommendations vary among vets, but 6 months of age is commonly suggested. Ask your vet what age is best for your Miniature Schnauzer.

Vaccinations

Another priority on a Miniature Schnauzer owner's list of preventive care is vaccinations. Vaccinations protect the dog against a host of infectious diseases, preventing an illness itself and the misery that accompanies it.

Vaccines should be a part of every young puppy's health care, since youngsters are so susceptible to disease. To remain effective, vaccinations must be kept current.

Good Nutrition

Dogs that receive the appropriate nutrients daily will be healthier and stronger than those that do not. The proper balance of proteins, fats, carbohydrates, vitamins, minerals and sufficient water enables the dog to remain healthy by fighting off illness.

Routine Checkups

Regular visits to the veterinary clinic should begin when your Miniature Schnauzer is a young pup and continue throughout his life. Make this a habit and it will certainly contribute to your Miniature Schnauzer's good health. Even if your Miniature Schnauzer seems perfectly healthy, a checkup once or twice a year is in order. Even if your dog seems fine to you, he could have an ongoing problem. Your veterinarian is trained to notice subtle changes or hints of illness.

Well-Being

Aside from the dog's physical needs—a proper and safe shelter, nutritious diet, health care and regular exercise—the Miniature Schnauzer needs plenty of plain, old-fashioned love. The dog is happiest when it is part of a family, enjoying the social interactions, nurturing and play. Bringing the Miniature Schnauzer into the family provides the dog with a sense of security.

The Miniature Schnauzer needs mental stimulation as well, especially because the breed is so intelligent. Obedience training is an excellent way to encourage your dog to use his mind. Remember, Miniature Schnauzers will use their brilliant minds in some manner, so it is best to direct them in a positive way.

Signs of Illness

Spotting illness in your Miniature Schnauzer early will go a long way toward a positive and safe prognosis. Actually recognizing specific signs of illness can be difficult, though. Owners must be sensitive to subtle, and sometimes not-so-subtle, signs that can indicate disease. Take note of the following list and be on the lookout for any of these:

- Changes in behavior. A normally outgoing dog may appear depressed and withdrawn.

- Changes in appetite, water intake, urination or bowel movements, temperament, heart rate and respiration rate.

23

Obedience training is fun and exciting for this Miniature Schnauzer, who is learning to heel.

- Apparent pain or sensitivity to touch.

- Dull hair coat or excessive hair loss.

- Weight loss.

- Vomiting or diarrhea.

- Blood in urine.

- Fever or runny nose and eyes.

- Swelling or lumps.

- Lethargy.

- Convulsions or choking.

- Unusual odor.

- Strained or shallow breathing.

COMMON DISEASES

Unfortunately, even with the best preventive care, the Miniature Schnauzer can fall ill. Infectious diseases, which are commonly spread from dog to dog via infected urine, feces or other body secretions, can wreak havoc. Following are a few of the diseases that can affect your Miniature Schnauzer.

Rabies

Rabies is preventable with routine vaccines, and such vaccinations are *required by law* for domestic animals in all states in this country. Given the seriousness of the disease, it would be foolish not to vaccinate your dog.

Probably one of the most well-known diseases that can affect dogs, rabies can strike any warm-blooded animal (including humans)—and is fatal. The rabies virus, which is present in an affected animal's saliva, is usually spread through a bite or open wound. The signs of the disease can be subtle at first. Normally friendly pets can become irritable and withdrawn. Shy pets may become overly friendly. Eventually, the dog becomes withdrawn and avoids light, which hurts the eyes of a rabid dog. Fever, vomiting and diarrhea are common.

Once these symptoms develop, the animal will die; there is no treatment or cure.

Since rabid animals may have a tendency to be aggressive and bite, animals suspected of having rabies should only be handled by animal control handlers or veterinarians.

Parvovirus

Canine parvovirus is a highly contagious and devastating illness. The

Diseases aren't a problem for these pups—they've had all their shots!

hardy virus is usually transmitted through contaminated feces, but it can be carried on an infected dog's feet or skin. It strikes dogs of all ages and is most serious in young puppies.

Young puppies receive antibody protection against the disease from their mother, but they lose it quickly and must be vaccinated to prevent the disease. In most cases, vaccinated puppies are protected against the disease.

There are two main types of parvovirus. The first signs of the diarrhea-syndrome type are usually depression and lack of appetite, followed by vomiting and the characteristic bloody diarrhea. The dog appears to be in great pain, and he usually has a high fever.

The cardiac-syndrome type affects the heart muscle and is most common in young puppies. Puppies with this condition will stop nursing, whine and gasp for air. Death may occur suddenly or in a few days. Youngsters that recover can have lingering heart failure that eventually takes their life.

Veterinarians can treat dogs with parvovirus, but the outcome varies. It depends on the age of the animal and severity of the disease, as well as on how much money an owner is willing to spend. Treatment may include fluid therapy, medication to stop the severe diarrhea and antibiotics to prevent or stop secondary infection. Treatment generally works—but it takes a long time and is considered emergency (expensive) treatment. Accordingly, it is best to vaccinate your dog to prevent it.

Coronavirus

Vaccinations against coronavirus are available to protect puppies and dogs against the virus and are recommended especially for all puppies and those dogs in frequent contact with other dogs.

Canine coronavirus is especially devastating to young puppies, causing depression, lack of appetite, vomiting that may contain blood and characteristically yellow-orange diarrhea. The virus is transmitted through feces, urine and saliva, and the onset of symptoms is usually rapid.

Dogs suffering from coronavirus are treated similarly to those suffering from parvovirus: fluid therapy, medication to stop diarrhea and vomiting and antibiotics if necessary.

Distemper

Caused by a virus, the highly contagious distemper used to be the leading cause of infectious disease in dogs. It is most common in unvaccinated puppies aged 3 to 8 months, but older dogs are susceptible as well.

The distemper virus frequently attacks the epithelial cells, which are found on the skin, eye membranes, breathing tubes and mucus membranes of the intestines. Some dogs become extremely ill and others do not. It often depends upon the dog's condition prior to illness.

The distemper virus is hardy and can live for many years. Incidence of distemper appears higher in the spring because the virus lies dormant in the earth, which is frozen during winter. Warm temperatures bring the spring thaw and reactivate the virus.

Distemper takes a variety of forms, and secondary infections and complications are common. Treatment is complex, and success varies.

The sooner the dog is treated, the better the prognosis.

Current vaccinations will prevent distemper in dogs, and it is especially important to vaccinate bitches before breeding to ensure maternal antibodies in the pups. In fact, vaccination has been so successful that veterinarians rarely see cases of distemper (about one per year or less).

Hepatitis

Infectious canine hepatitis can affect dogs of every age, but it is most severe in puppies. It primarily affects the dog's liver, kidneys and lining of the blood vessels. Highly contagious, it is transmitted through urine, feces and saliva.

This disease has several forms. In the fatal fulminating form, the dog becomes ill very suddenly, develops bloody diarrhea and dies. In the acute form, the dog develops a fever, has bloody diarrhea, vomits blood and refuses to eat. Jaundice may be present; the whites of the dog's eyes appear yellow. Dogs with a mild case are lethargic or depressed and often refuse to eat.

Infectious canine hepatitis must be diagnosed and confirmed with a blood test. Ill dogs require hospitalization. Hepatitis is preventable in dogs by keeping vaccinations current.

Lyme Disease

Lyme disease has received a lot of press recently, with its increased incidence throughout the United States. The illness, caused by the bacteria *Borrelia burgdorferi,* is carried by ticks. It is passed along when the tick bites a victim, canine or human. (The dog cannot pass the disease to people, though. It is only transmitted via the tick.) It is most common during the tick season from May through August.

In dogs, the disease manifests itself in sudden lameness, caused by swollen joints, similar to arthritis. The dog is weak and may run a fever. The lameness can last a few days or several months, and some dogs have recurring difficulties.

27

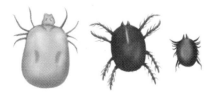

Three types of ticks (l-r): the wood tick, brown dog tick and deer tick.

POISON ALERT

If your dog has ingested a potentially poisonous substance, waste no time. Call the National Animal Poison Control Center hot line:

(800) 548-2423 ($30 per case) or

(900) 680-0000 ($20 first five minutes; $2.95 each additional minute)

Antibiotics are very effective in treating Lyme disease, and the sooner it is diagnosed and treated, the better. A vaccine is available; ask your veterinarian if your dog would benefit from it.

Kennel Cough

"Kennel cough," or the more politically correct "canine cough," is a contagious disease that shows itself as a harsh, dry cough. It has been termed "kennel cough," because of its often rapid spread through kennels. The cough may persist for weeks and is often followed by a bout of chronic bronchitis.

Many kennels require proof of bordatella vaccination before boarding. If your dog is in and out of kennels frequently, vaccination certainly is not a bad idea.

FIRST AID

First aid is not a substitute for professional care, though it can help save a dog's life.

To Stop Bleeding

Bleeding from a severe cut or wound must be stopped right away. There are two basic techniques—direct pressure and the tourniquet.

Try to control bleeding first by using direct pressure. Ask an assistant to hold the injured Miniature Schnauzer and place several pads of sterile gauze over the wound. Press. Do not wipe the wound or apply any cleansers or ointments. Apply firm, even pressure. If blood soaks through the pad, do not remove it as this could disrupt clotting. Simply place another pad on top and continue to apply pressure.

If bleeding on a leg or the tail does not stop by applying pressure, try using a tourniquet. Use this only as a last resort. A tourniquet that is left on too long can result in limb loss.

If the dog is bleeding from his mouth or vomits or defecates blood, he may be suffering from internal injuries. Do not attempt to stop bleeding. Call the veterinarian right away for emergency treatment.

Shock

Whenever a dog is injured or is seriously ill, the odds are good that he will go into a state of shock. A decreased supply of oxygen to the tissues usually results in unconsciousness; pale gums; weak, rapid pulse and labored, rapid breathing. If not treated, a dog will die from shock. The conditions of the dog should continue to be treated, but the dog should be as comfortable as possible. A blanket can help keep a dog warm. A dog in shock needs immediate veterinary care.

Heatstroke

Heatstroke can be deadly and must be treated immediately to save the dog. Signs include rapid panting, darker-than-usual gums and tongue, salivating, exhaustion or vomiting. The dog's body temperature is elevated, sometimes as high as 106°F. If the dog is not treated, coma and death can follow.

If heatstroke is suspected, cool down your overheated dog as quickly as possible. Take your dog's

WHEN TO CALL THE VETERINARIAN

In any emergency situation, you should call your veterinarian immediately. Try to stay calm when you call, and give the vet or the assistant as much information as possible before you leave for the clinic. That way, the staff will be able to take immediate, specific action when you arrive. Emergencies include:

- Bleeding or deep wounds
- Hyperthermia (overheating)
- Shock
- Dehydration
- Abdominal Pain
- Burns
- Fits
- Unconsciousness
- Broken bones
- Paralysis

Call your veterinarian if you suspect any health troubles.

temperature. If it is over 104°F or if your dog seems unsteady, he must be cooled by immersion in a tub of cool water or hosed down with a garden hose. For a temperature over 106°F or if your dog seems ready to collapse, a cool water enema is in order. The idea is to drop the dog's body temperature rapidly. Mildly affected dogs can be moved to a cooler environment, into an air-conditioned home, for example, or wrapped in moistened towels.

Insect Bites/Stings

Just like people, dogs can suffer bee stings and insect bites. Bees, wasps and yellow jackets leave a nasty, painful sting, and if your dog is stung repeatedly, shock can occur.

If an insect bite is suspected, try to identify the culprit. Remove the

In routine vet visits, the doctor will check your Miniature Schnauzer's eyes, ears, teeth and whole body.

stinger, if it is a bee sting, and apply a mixture of baking soda and water to the sting. It is also a good idea to apply ice packs to reduce inflammation and ease pain. Call your veterinarian, especially if your dog seems ill or goes into shock.

INTERNAL PARASITES

Dogs are susceptible to several internal parasites. Keeping your Miniature Schnauzer free of internal parasites is another important aspect of health care.

Watch for general signs of poor condition: a dull haircoat, weight loss, lethargy, coughing, weakness and diarrhea.

Roundworms

Roundworms, or ascarids, are probably the most common worms that affect dogs. Most puppies are born with these organisms in their intestines, which is why youngsters are treated for these parasites as soon as it is safe to do so.

Dogs usually contract roundworms by ingesting infested soil or feces. A roundworm infestation can rob vital nutrients from young puppies and cause diarrhea, vomiting and digestive upset. Roundworms can also harm a young animal's liver and lungs, so treatment is imperative.

Tapeworms

Tapeworms are commonly transmitted by fleas to dogs. Tapeworm eggs enter the body of a canine host when the animal accidentally ingests a carrier flea. The parasite settles in the intestines, where it sinks its head into the intestinal wall and feeds off material the host is digesting. The worm grows a body of egg packets, which break off periodically and are expelled from the body in the feces. Fleas then ingest the eggs from the feces and the parasite's life cycle begins all over again.

Hookworms

Hookworms are so named because they hook onto an animal's small intestine and suck the host's blood. Like roundworms, hookworms are contracted when a dog ingests contaminated soil or feces.

Hookworms can be especially devastating to dogs. They will

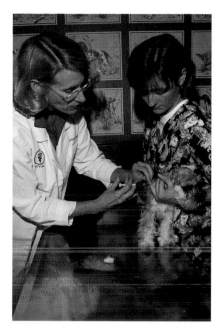

It is important to schedule regular veterinary visits to stay current in vaccines.

become thin and sick; puppies can die. An affected dog will suffer from bloody diarrhea and, if the parasites migrate to the lungs, the dog may contract bronchitis or pneumonia.

Hookworms commonly strike puppies 2 to 8 weeks of age and are less common in adult dogs.

Whipworms

Known for their thread-like appearance, whipworms attach into the wall of the large intestine to feed. Thick-shelled eggs are passed in the

WHAT'S WRONG WITH MY DOG?

We've listed some common conditions of health problems and their possible causes. If any of the following conditions appear serious or persist for more than 24 hours, make an appointment to see your veterinarian immediately.

CONDITIONS	POSSIBLE CAUSES
DIARRHEA	Intestinal upset, typically caused by eating something bad or overeating. Can also be a viral infection, a bad case of nerves or anxiety or a parasite infection. If you see blood in the feces, get to the vet right away.
VOMITING/RETCHING	Dogs regurgitate fairly regularly (bitches for their young), whenever something upsets their stomach, or even out of excitement or anxiety. Often dogs eat grass, which, because it's indigestible in its pure form, irritates their stomachs and causes them to vomit. Getting a good look at *what* your dog vomited can better indicate what's causing it.
COUGHING	Obstruction in the throat; virus (kennel cough); roundworm infestation; congestive heart failure.
RUNNY NOSE	Because dogs don't catch colds like people, a runny nose is a sign of congestion or irritation.
LOSS OF APPETITE	Because most dogs are hearty and regular eaters, a loss of appetite can be your first and most accurate sign of a serious problem.
LOSS OF ENERGY (LETHARGY)	Any number of things could be slowing down your dog, from an infection to internal tumors to overexercise—even overeating.

feces and in about two to four weeks are mature and able to reinfect a host that ingests the eggs.

Mild whipworm infestation is often without signs, but as the worms grow, weight loss, bloody diarrhea and anemia follow. In areas where the soil is heavily contaminated, frequent checks are advised to prevent severe infestation.

CONDITIONS	POSSIBLE CAUSES
STINKY BREATH	Imagine if you never brushed your teeth! Foul-smelling breath indicates plaque and tartar buildup that could possibly have caused infection. Start brushing your dog's teeth.
LIMPING	This could be caused by something as simple as a hurt or bruised pad, to something as complicated as hip dysplasia, torn ligaments or broken bones.
CONSTANT ITCHING	Probably due to fleas, mites or an allergic reaction to food or environment (your vet will need to help you determine what your dog's allergic to).
RED, INFLAMED, ITCHY SPOTS	Often referred to as "hot spots," these are particularly common on coated breeds. They're caused by a bacterial infection that gets aggravated as the dog licks and bites at the spot.
BALD SPOTS	These are the result of excessive itching or biting at the skin so that the hair follicles are damaged; excessively dry skin; mange; calluses; and even infections. You need to determine what the underlying cause is.
STINKY EARS/HEAD SHAKING	Take a look under your dog's ear flap. Do you see brown, waxy buildup? Clean the ears with something soft and a special cleaner, and don't use cotton swabs or go too deep into the ear canal.
UNUSUAL LUMPS	Could be fatty tissue, could be something serious (infection, trauma, tumor). Don't wait to find out.

33

Heartworms

Heartworms are transmitted by the ordinary mosquito, but the effects are far from ordinary. Infection begins when the larvae from an infected mosquito are laid on the dog's skin. They burrow into the skin, or are ingested when the dog licks. In three to four months, the

FLEAS AND TICKS

There are so many safe, effective products available now to combat fleas and ticks that—thankfully—they are less of a problem. Prevention is key, however. Ask your veterinarian about starting your puppy on a flea/tick repellant right away. With this, regular grooming and environmental controls, your dog and your home should stay pest-free. Without this attention, you risk infesting your dog and your home, and you're in for an ugly and costly battle to clear up the problem.

larvae (microfilaria) become small worms and make their way to a vein, where they are transported to the heart. The worms burrow into the heart, grow and reproduce.

At first, a dog with heartworms is free of symptoms. The signs vary, but the most common is a deep cough and shortness of breath. The dog tires easily, is weak and loses weight. Eventually, the dog may suffer from congestive heart failure.

EXTERNAL PARASITES

FLEAS—Besides carrying tapeworm larvae, fleas bite and suck the host's blood. Their bites itch and are extremely annoying to dogs, especially if the dog is hypersensitive to the bite. Fleas must be eliminated on the dog with special shampoos and dips. Fleas also infest the dog's bedding and the owner's home and yard.

TICKS—Several varieties of ticks attach themselves to dogs, where they burrow into the skin and suck blood. Ticks can be carriers of several diseases, including Lyme disease and Rocky Mountain Spotted Fever.

LICE—Lice are not common in dogs, but when they are present they cause intense irritation and itching. There are two types: biting and sucking. Biting lice feed on skin scales, and sucking lice feed on blood.

MITES—There are several types of mites that cause several kinds of mange, including sarcoptic, demodectic and cheyletiella. These microscopic mites cause intense itching and misery to the dog.

CHAPTER FOUR

Positively Nutritious

NUTRITIONAL NEEDS

The Miniature Schnauzer's body requires certain substances that she cannot manufacture herself; she must get these from the food she eats. Eventually, poor nutrition shows up as skin problems, dull, dry coat, poor stools, behavior problems, immune system deficiencies, susceptibility to disease and, eventually, a much shorter life span. A dog that is fed a balanced diet will have a shiny coat, bright eyes and lots of energy.

HOW MANY MEALS A DAY?

Individual dogs vary in how much they should eat to maintain a desired body weight—not too fat, but not too thin. Puppies need several meals a day, while older dogs may need only one. Determine how much food keeps your adult dog looking and feeling her best. Then decide how many meals you want to feed with that amount. Like us, most dogs love to eat, and offering two meals a day is more enjoyable for them. If you're worried about overfeeding, make sure you measure correctly and abstain from adding tidbits to the meals.

Whether you feed one or two meals, only leave your dog's food out for the amount of time it takes her to eat it—ten minutes, for example. Free-feeding (when food is available any time) and leisurely meals encourage picky eating. Don't worry if your dog doesn't finish all her dinner in the allotted time. She'll learn she should.

QUALITY VARIES

A good quality food is necessary for your Miniature Schnauzer's health. To make sure you are using a high-quality food, read the labels on the dog-food package (see the sidebar, "How to Read the Dog Food Label"). Make sure the food offers balanced levels of proteins, carbohydrates and fats.

HOW MUCH TO FEED A PUPPY

During her period of intense growth and development between birth and 6 months, a puppy requires almost twice the amount of most nutrients per pound of body weight compared to an adult dog's needs. At 6 to 8 weeks of age, a puppy requires at least three times the adult dog's caloric requirements per pound of body weight. Because of these nutritional needs, you should feed your puppy three or four times a day. Ask your veterinarian or breeder how much per meal; you don't want your puppy to eat too much, but you certainly don't want to underfeed her.

This caloric requirement gradually decreases to twice the adult dog's needs until the puppy is 16 weeks old and continues to gradually decrease, reaching an adult dog's caloric requirement at about 1 year of age. The number of meals you feed will decrease, too, until your puppy is eating one or two meals a day.

Manufacturers of the best brands of puppy food have taken all of these requirements into consideration, and since the amounts fed to your puppy gradually decrease over her growth and development period, the decreased caloric ingestion is automatic. During that first intensive year, a nutritional and balanced diet will develop strong bones and teeth, clear eyes and a healthy coat and will promote healthy body functions.

YOUR PUPPY'S FEEDING ROUTINE

Your puppy's food bowl and water container should be placed where they are clearly visible to you, but out of the path of foot traffic. Both

FOOD ALLERGIES

If your puppy or dog seems to itch all the time for no apparent reason, she could be allergic to one or more ingredients in her food. This is not uncommon, and it's why many foods contain lamb and rice instead of beef, wheat or soy. Have your dog tested by your veterinarian, and be patient while you strive to identify and eliminate the allergens from your dog's food (or environment).

containers should be scrubbed frequently to avoid bacterial contamination. Fresh, clean water should be

Active puppies burn more calories, which is why they require a higher caloric intake and extra nutrients.

How to Read the Dog Food Label

With so many choices on the market, how can you be sure you are feeding the right food to your dog? The information is all there on the label—if you know what you're looking for.

Look for the nutritional claim right up top. Is the food "100 percent nutritionally complete"? If so, it's for nearly all life stages; "growth and maintenance," on the other hand, is for early development; puppy foods are marked as such, as are foods for senior dogs.

Ingredients are listed in descending order by weight. The first three or four ingredients will tell you the bulk of what the food contains. Look for the highest-quality ingredients, like meats and grains, to be among them.

The Guaranteed Analysis tells you what levels of protein, fat, fiber and moisture are in the food, in that order. While these numbers are meaningful, they won't tell you much about the quality of the food. Nutritional value is in the dry matter, not the moisture content.

In many ways, seeing is believing. If your dog has bright eyes, a shiny coat, a good appetite and a good energy level, chances are her diet's fine. Your dog's breeder and your veterinarian are good sources of advice if you're still confused.

available to your puppy—and throughout her adult life—at all times.

You have two choices of feeding routines: scheduled feedings (allowing you to determine her mealtimes) or self-feeding (allowing her to determine her mealtimes). Scheduled feedings are preferable. They make for easier housetraining (keeping in mind the rule that what goes in must come out fairly soon afterward) and, in the long run, a healthier dog. Self-fed dogs tend to be fussier, so you may not recognize a loss of appetite as a health problem until it's serious, whereas if your normally eager-to-eat Miniature Schnauzer won't eat, you'll know there's a problem right away.

Discourage Fussy Eating

So your dog doesn't develop a fussiness problem, the best thing to do is keep to a feeding schedule, put her bowl down and leave it down for ten to fifteen minutes at the most. If she's not finished eating in that time, remove the extra food. Do not let it sit out so she can eat it at her leisure. When mealtime comes around again, feed the normal amount and use the same rules. She'll learn that if she wants all her dinner, she'd better eat it right away. And you'll learn when she's not feeling well by how much she's eating.

While a roly-poly puppy is cute and healthy, don't allow her to become an obese adult by overfeeding or through lack of exercise. If she does become overweight, decrease the amount of food she's offered until she's the correct weight, then maintain the proper amount of food, and make sure she gets plenty of exercise.

AVOID BAD TABLE MANNERS

If you're annoyed by the interruption of telephone sales pitches at dinner time, you'll be more annoyed by your dog pestering you during your meals. To avoid her pesky behavior, you mustn't allow it. The first time she places her paws on your lap, your immediate reaction must be a stern "Off" as you push her away. You're not angry; your attitude is quite matter-of-fact as you continue to eat. She'll probably try again, placing her paws on your lap. As many times as necessary continue to push her away with a stern "Off," exhibiting your

TO SUPPLEMENT OR NOT TO SUPPLEMENT?

If you're feeding your dog a diet that's correct for her developmental stage and she's alert, healthy looking and neither over- nor underweight, you don't need to add supplements. These include table scraps as well as vitamins and minerals. In fact, unless you are a nutrition expert, using food supplements can actually hurt a growing puppy. For example, mixing too much calcium into your dog's food can lead to musculoskeletal disorders. Educating yourself about the quantity of vitamins and minerals your dog needs to be healthy will help you determine what needs to be supplemented. If you have any concerns about the nutritional quality of the food you're feeding, discuss them with your veterinarian.

Your healthy Miniature Schnauzer has bright eyes, a shiny coat and lots of energy.

TYPES OF FOODS/TREATS

There are three types of commercially available dog food—dry, canned and semimoist—and a huge assortment of treats (lucky dogs!) to feed your dog. Which should you choose?

Dry and canned foods contain similar ingredients. The primary difference between them is their moisture content. The moisture is not just water. It's blood and broth, too, the very things that dogs adore. So while canned food is more palatable, dry food is more economical, convenient and effective in controlling tartar buildup. Most owners feed a 25 percent canned/75 percent dry diet to give their dogs the benefit of both. Just be sure your dog is getting the nutrition she needs (you and your veterinarian can determine this).

Semimoist foods have the flavor dogs love and the convenience owners want. However, they tend to contain excessive amounts of artificial colors and preservatives.

Dog treats come in every size, shape and flavor imaginable, from organic cookies shaped like postmen to beefy chew sticks. Dogs seem to love them all, so enjoy the variety. Just be sure not to overindulge your dog. Factor treats into her regular meal sizes.

will only be subjected to your consistent reaction.

When you're convinced, after months of your puppy's proper behavior and no bothersome paws on your lap, that she's reliable, sneak a piece of meat on the table edge and see if she attempts to swipe it. If she does, you know what you must do. Sometime later, try to trap her again, and if she ignores the bait, praise her, but under no circumstances should she be rewarded (at least at that moment) by giving her the meat treat.

Persistent whining or barking during your mealtime may be corrected with your "No" accompanied by a shake of a can filled with coins or something else unpleasant. She must learn what behaviors are and are not acceptable, and you must always be alert and ready for corrections with the can's use. The cooperation of every family member must be made clear. If you've managed to teach her not to pester you while others are sneaking table scraps to her, the poor puppy will be utterly confused, wondering why you're so mean to her.

Children, especially, must learn not to "accidentally" drop bits of

unchanged attitude until she simply gives up. She may try again during that meal or the next or the next, but

food on the floor. They'll feel quite satisfied if they're encouraged to wait until a later time after each meal when they may offer a treat to the puppy. Let them join in the puppy's training, but under your supervision.

Offering treats to your Miniature Schnauzer is a great way to add a little variety to her diet!

SNACKS

An occasional dog biscuit or training treat will not spoil your Miniature Schnauzer's appetite, but don't get into the habit of offering treats. Many American dogs are overweight, and obesity is a leading killer of dogs. When you do offer treats, offer either treats made specifically for dogs or something low in calories and nutritious, like a carrot. Don't offer candy, cookies, leftover tacos or anything like that. Your Miniature Schnauzer doesn't need sugar, and chocolate is deadly for dogs. Spicy foods can cause diarrhea and an upset stomach. Play it safe and give your Miniature Schnauzer good quality, nutritious snacks very sparingly.

41

CHAPTER FIVE

Putting on the Dog

Your time and trouble, however, are worth the effort; consider the result. Gloat, if you must!

GROOMING EQUIPMENT

Even though you may have your Miniature Schnauzer groomed at a commercial establishment, you'll need to maintain his appearance between visits. A grooming table, whether homemade or purchased, is ideal for the procedure if it's fitted with an adjustable post, but a rubber bath mat or any nonslip surface placed on a table may be substituted. Proper lighting is essential. A smooth-surfaced doctor's jacket, nurse's uniform or grooming smock

P ossibly considering your friends to be "stuck" with their shedding, smelly breeds, you'd better withhold your temptation to gloat. Your Miniature Schnauzer's ideal, non-shedding, non-smelling coat doesn't just sit there looking beautiful without attention given to it.

is ideal clothing for you. The grooming tools you'll need are a slicker brush, coarse-toothed comb, hemostat, nail clippers and a canine nail file, all of which you must regularly disinfect.

If you clip your dog yourself, scissors and electric clipper blades should be sharpened by a reputable shop specializing in the maintenance of grooming tools. Treat your tools with respect; dropping them on the floor will force them out of alignment. The ideal bathing facility will be an appropriately sized tub with a spray hose; less ideal, one tub for shampooing and another for rinsing with a plastic cup or dipper. The dog should be bathed with a quality shampoo especially formulated for dogs, and the nail clippers should be suitable for a medium-size dog. Equipment to strip a show coat should be discussed with the person who will help you with the procedure.

PREPARING YOUR PUPPY FOR GROOMING

Since grooming will become a regular and daily part of your Miniature Schnauzer's life, teach him to stand

GROOMING TOOLS

pin brush	scissors
slicker brush	nail clippers
flea comb	tooth-cleaning equipment
towel	shampoo
mat rake	conditioner
grooming glove	clippers

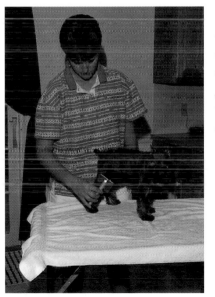

This Miniature Schnauzer stands comfortably on a grooming table while being brushed.

43

for very short periods by holding him up under his tummy while you stroke and softly praise him, saying, "Stand." If he wiggles (and he will), patiently continue the procedure for a moment, then stop. He's learning,

Getting your Miniature Schnauzer to look as sharp as these champions takes time, patience and lots of practice.

44

and you don't want to push him to the limit. If he tries to sit (and he will), gently lift him under his tummy and remind him to "Stand." When the puppy is comfortably and agreeably content to remain standing for a while, gradually extend the time.

EYE, TOENAIL AND EAR CARE

Every day, check your Miniature Schnauzer's eyes because many dogs accumulate a bit of mucus in the corner of each one. Use a tissue or cotton ball to remove any matter, or wipe the area with a product specifically made for eye tearing, then rinse with clear water.

Your dog's toenails must be trimmed or they'll curl into a discomforting length that will not permit him to walk properly on the pads of his feet. If clicking is heard as he walks, his nails are too long.

Any scissors may be used for a very young puppy, but commercial nail clippers are necessary when the nails grow thicker. Two types are available: the pliers and the guillotine. The latter is recommended since it's designed to enable you to see how much you're cutting, and the most popular brand has a replaceable blade. Always have a blood coagulant ready in the event you cut the "quick" (the vein that runs through the center of each nail). Pet shops carry a styptic powder product that quickly stops the bleeding when the nail is dipped into it, or you may use a silver nitrate stick. You'll be cutting a lot of nails throughout the dog's life, and it's inevitable that you'll cut a quick. Apply the coagulant, and stop feeling guilty.

NAIL-CLIPPING TIPS

You'll also need a nail file specially designed for dogs' nails. Lift a foot and allow it to rest on your hand with your thumb stroking the top. Do not tightly grip the foot or pull the leg; you'll only cause resentment, resistance and refusal to cooperate.

If you introduce the procedure slowly, patiently and gently, the puppy will be more cooperative. If the hair on his foot covers his nails, making it difficult for you to see them, wet your thumb and push the hair back to expose the nail (or poke the nails through an old nylon stocking).

When using the nail clippers, hold them according to the packaging directions. At a point just below the bend of the nail, cut each nail at a slight upward angle toward the dog. Round off each nail with the nail file. If the nails ever grow too long, clip them as short as possible just beyond the quick, then file the tips every other day (which will force the quick to recede) until the nails are the correct length.

TENDING THE EARS

Since the Miniature Schnauzer is a breed whose coat continually grows, the ears require constant watch. The hair inside the ears, if not removed, will grow downward into the ear canal. Canine products specifically manufactured for the care of ears

QUICK AND PAINLESS NAIL CLIPPING

This is possible if you make a habit out of handling your dog's feet and giving your dog treats when you do. When it's time to clip nails, go through the same routine, but take your clippers and snip off just the ends of the nail—clip too far down and you'll cut into the "quick," the nerve center, hurting your dog and causing the nail to bleed. Clip two nails a session while you're getting your dog used to the procedure, and you'll soon be doing all four feet quickly and easily.

45

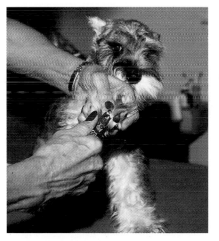

This Miniature Schnauzer was taught at a young age to sit calmly for his nail clipping.

include powders, liquid cleansing solutions and odor reducers.

If your dog is groomed professionally, be sure that the groomer

It is essential to incorporate ear hair removal into your dog's regular grooming regimen.

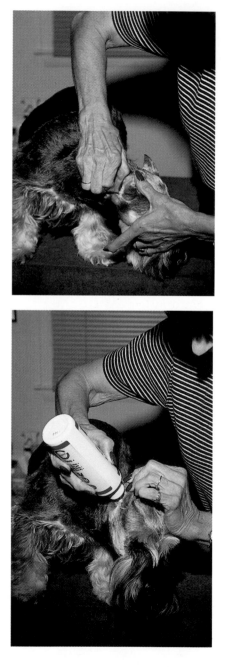

This owner loosens dirt and wax from her dog's ear with a commercial canine ear cleanser.

completes the procedure on each visit. If you groom your dog yourself, you'll be responsible for its undertaking. Sprinkle some powder into the ear and fluff it around by gently tapping the ear's surface with your forefinger. Your dog will be manageable if you hold his head gently against your body with your free hand.

The powder's purpose is to allow your thumb and forefinger to grasp and pull out the easily visible hairs inside the ear near the surface. Be sure to remove only a few hairs at a time or you'll cause pain. Continue to withdraw the hair until that part of the ear has been cleared of hair. Spreading the ear will enable you to see the hair growing deeper inside the ear. If necessary, add more powder.

Using a hemostat (an invaluable tool), grasp a few strands of hair and withdraw them. Be careful with the hemostat; avoid poking the skin or grasping a bit of flesh with it. After the ear is cleared of hair, the powder must be removed or it will accumulate bacteria. Using a cotton ball or a cotton swab dipped into baby lotion (but not dripping with it), gently wipe the inside of the ear. Anytime hair accumulates, it must be removed.

Whether your dog is groomed professionally or by you, regularly check the ears for any wax or dirt that has accumulated—a normal expectancy. Place three or four drops of a commercial canine ear cleansing solution into the ear and massage the ear at the base for three minutes to distribute the solution. With a series of cotton swabs, gently cleanse the ear, removing all of the accumulated debris. Then use a cotton ball to remove all of the liquid solution.

CARING FOR TEETH AND GUMS

Like all dogs, adult Miniature Schnauzers have forty-two permanent teeth; puppies have twenty-three baby teeth with no molars. As each adult tooth emerges, any interfering baby tooth should be removed.

You should make it a habit to examine your dog's mouth several times a week. Tartar and plaque develop on dogs' teeth the same way they do on ours. Tartar is a hard, yellow-brown or gray-white deposit on the teeth and cannot be removed by brushing; it must be removed professionally by your veterinarian. Tartar develops from plaque, a soft white or yellow substance.

Buildup of either causes gingivitis and results in gums that are red, sensitive, swollen and sore. When

47

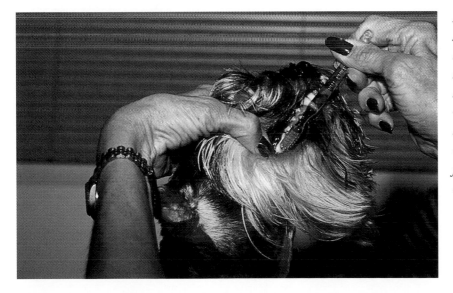

Keeping your Miniature Schnauzer's teeth and gums healthy is easy with regular brushing—and it's not so bad for his breath either!

rubbed, the gums may bleed. The gums separate from the sides of the teeth, allowing bacteria and food to collect inside, which invites periodontal disease.

If you want your dog to have healthy teeth all his life, and to avoid serious oral infections, the tartar on his teeth must be removed whenever it begins to accumulate. Some dogs, regardless of their diet, require less frequent tartar removal than others, who are extremely prone to an ongoing collection. The appearance of an adult dog's sparkling white front teeth is deceptive; his back teeth (and the inside of those front teeth) may have a collection of tartar, causing the gums to swell and possibly become infected, and the teeth to decay.

DOG BREATH—If your dog has gingivitis, what you'll probably notice first is offensive dog breath. Dog breath is a sure sign you've neglected your dog's tooth care. If you haven't, and your dog's teeth are healthy, it's a sign of another problem. In either event, you should make an appointment to see your veterinarian.

Tartar can be easily removed by regular brushing of your dog's teeth at home. Use a toothbrush designed for dogs, a child's soft toothbrush or a gauze pad wrapped around your finger. Use toothpaste specifically formulated for dogs, not human toothpaste, which is bad for dogs.

"Brush" your dog's teeth by rubbing the toothpaste along the gum line and over the surface of the teeth. Do this two or three times a week (daily is preferable) as prescribed in the product's directions. There's no need to rinse. Dog toothpastes taste good to dogs, and will be rinsed and swallowed by drinking water in the course of the day.

COAT CARE

Your Miniature Schnauzer should be brushed daily; minimally two or three times a week. When his puppy coat is long enough to groom, gently brush it with a slicker brush, which has wire bristles that bend. With your fingers, remove any burs or foreign matter from his coat. Mats, which are knotted hairs, should be separated by your fingers and the end teeth of a coarse comb into smaller and smaller sections until a comb may be drawn through them.

While being careful to avoid digging the bristles into the skin, the coat must be brushed thoroughly from the skin outward, not merely the coat's surface. The coat first is brushed in the direction in which it grows, then in the opposite direction, and finally again in the direction in which it grows. This procedure will remove dirt and loose skin particles, stimulate circulation and secretion of the natural skin oils and ensure a healthy coat.

The furnishings of each leg are brushed in a downward direction, starting at the feet, then moving upward to the next layer and the next layer, until the entire leg is brushed. It is rebrushed in an upward direction, and again downward.

The beard and moustache are brushed starting at the outer edge, moving to the next layer, etc., until you've reached the skin. You will then "proof" your brushing by combing everything with a coarse-toothed comb. An adult Miniature Schnauzer with a clipped coat needs so little maintenance that he can have a spiffy appearance every day of his life. A daily brushing of four legs, two eyebrows, a beard and a mustache is a small investment of time for such a great return.

A relaxing daily brushing will prevent mats and knotted hairs from taunting your Miniature Schnauzer.

49

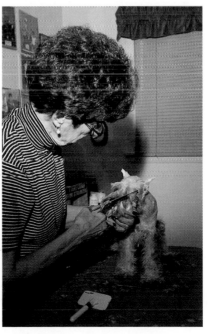

Don't forget to put the finishing touches on your Miniature Schnauzer's eyebrows, beard and moustache.

THE BATH

Any bath must be preceded by a thorough brushing and combing of your dog's coat. Thoroughly soak him with warm (not hot) water and place a small bit of absorbent cotton in each ear. When your Miniature Schnauzer is thoroughly wet, work up a lather on his back with shampoo and briskly rub his coat. Remove the cotton from his ears, then, without using shampoo, wash them inside and out with a clean, dampened and wrung-out washcloth and place fresh cotton in each ear. Again avoiding water in his eyes and ears, thoroughly rinse him with warm, not hot, water until no trace

This dog's coat was thoroughly brushed before his bath.

of shampoo remains in his coat. Then rinse again! If it is necessary, bathe and rinse him again.

Quickly squeeze the excess water from the puppy's coat and place him in a towel to absorb as much moisture as possible. Towel-dry him with another towel (or blow-dry him with an electric hair dryer) until he is barely damp. With a clean brush and comb, groom his coat to make sure that it is free from mats.

THE CLIPPED COAT

If you decide to clip your dog, study the procedure; learn from an experienced friend, breeder or other helpful soul, then enjoy a permanently (and less expensively) maintained Miniature Schnauzer. The clipped coat pattern is relatively easy to learn and simple to perform.

THE SHOW COAT

Maintaining your Miniature Schnauzer in a stripped coat is not easy, and it is not likely that a commercial groomer will know the procedure or be willing to accept the challenge. You will have to learn from an exhibitor, breeder or professional handler. Perhaps one will allow you to watch the procedure and teach you the technique. Not only is it intricate and time-consuming, it must be done in several stages and be precisely timed for each show season.

The stripped show coat displays the Miniature Schnauzer in his most typically attractive appearance, but the periods between a "blown" show coat and his next new show coat are lengthy and create an almost unattractive appearance. Your lifestyle, time, energy and needs must determine which appearance is the more suitable for you.

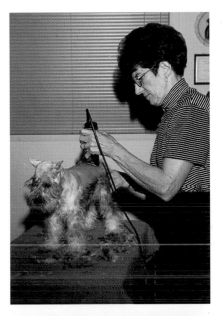

A clipped coat is neat and clean—and easy to learn how to do.

Maintaining a show coat takes time and energy—but is well worth it!

CHAPTER SIX

Measuring Up

without being froufrou; highly protective yet underwhelming in size; and equipped with the bonus of all bonuses, a non-shedding coat with no trace of a doggy odor.

THE DOG'S QUALITY

There are two types of dogs available to the buyer: pet quality and show quality. A Miniature Schnauzer of pet quality is deemed so because she either has a disqualification or a fault as described by the breed standard. She may have a coat too soft in texture or an improper bite, be too large or too small or lack any quality required—but in no way is she less desirable as a companion.

D istinctive" is the word that most accurately describes the Miniature Schnauzer, for she is very affectionate without being overbearingly gushy; highly intelligent with some degree of independence; extremely curious but not destructive; elegant in appearance

Pet-quality dogs are usually available for a lower price than show quality, but it sometimes happens that a breeder is left with an unsold show-quality prospect he cannot keep. Its gender may not be what the breeder wanted; another litter may be on the way, creating a time or space problem for the breeder; the puppy's fault (remember, she's not perfect) may be one the breeder must avoid. For whatever reason, the breeder may sell a show-quality prospect at a pet price.

UNDERSTANDING THE BREED STANDARD

The following is a discussion of the elements of the breed standard for the Miniature Schnauzer. To get a copy of the official breed standard, write to the American Kennel Club or visit it on-line. Ask specifically for the Miniature Schnauzer Standard.

General Appearance and Temperament

The standard's description of the Miniature Schnauzer's general

WHAT IS A BREED STANDARD?

A breed standard—a detailed description of an individual breed—is meant to portray the ideal specimen of that breed. This includes ideal structure, temperament, gait, type—all aspects of the dog. Because the standard describes an ideal specimen, it isn't based on any particular dog. It is a concept against which judges compare actual dogs and breeders strive to produce dogs. At a dog show, the dog that wins is the one that comes closest, in the judge's opinion, to the standard for its breed. Breed standards are written by the breed parent clubs, the national organizations formed to oversee the well-being of the breed. They are voted on and approved by the members of the parent clubs.

53

appearance depicts no fluffy, cutesy little dog. Rather, she is a classy lady. A puppy easily falls into the little fluff-of-a-dog slot, but those sturdy bones and squarish body, even at a young age, predict the robust and proportionately impressive adult who somehow replaces the fluff.

The standard's ideal temperament (describing an alert, spirited, obedient, friendly, intelligent dog with a willingness to please) is abundantly evident in the typical Miniature Schnauzer.

*The Miniature
Schnauzer
carries herself
with dignity.*

Head

A good Miniature Schnauzer head is a beauty to behold, and balance is the key, particularly if the head is in balance with the rest of the dog. The unwrinkled forehead enhances the flat and fairly long topskull (the area behind the eyes) ending at a slight stop (the indentation between the eyes where the nasal bone and skull meet).

The foreface (the area in front of the eyes) is strong and at least as long as the topskull. Both parts (foreface and muzzle) are parallel to each other, separated by the stop. Thick whiskers accentuate the rectangular shape of the head. A head that is coarse (lacking refinement) and cheeky (prominently rounded, thick, protruding) is a no-no. A scissors bite (fully defined in the standard) is required.

The keen expression of the small, dark brown, deeply set, oval-shaped eyes almost resembles a frown, which perhaps conceals the dog's studied contemplation of her next move.

Ears

If the ears are cropped (if a portion of the ears have been surgically removed), they must be identical in shape and length with pointed tips, in balance with the head, set high on the skull, carried perpendicularly at the inner edge and they must stand erect. Uncropped (natural) ears must be small, must be V-shaped and fold close to the skull.

Body

The Miniature Schnauzer's body should be very square. The length from the chest (the front of the dog beneath the head and neck) to the stern (tail) bone should be equal to the height, measured from the floor (or wherever she is stood) to her withers (the highest point on the shoulders, immediately behind the neck). Ribs are well sprung and deep (the opposite of a slender, flat-sided dog). The brisket (the foreport of the body below the chest, between the forelegs, closest to the ribs) should extend at least to the elbows. While robustness is desirable, too much is as bad as too little.

The topline (the topmost outline of the dog from just behind the withers to the tail set) should be straight, declining at a slight angle as it travels from the neck to the tail. A topline is faulted if it is sway-back (a concave or hollow curvature

The breed's keen expression almost resembles a frown.

55

This Miniature Schnauzer's relatively "square" body measures up to the breed standard.

THE AMERICAN KENNEL CLUB

Familiarly referred to as "the AKC," the American Kennel Club is a nonprofit organization devoted to the advancement of purebred dogs. The AKC maintains a registry of recognized breeds and adopts and enforces rules for dog events including shows, obedience trials, field trials, hunting tests, lure coursing, herding, earthdog trials, agility and the Canine Good Citizen program. It is a club of clubs, established in 1884 and composed, today, of over 500 autonomous dog clubs throughout the United States. Each club is represented by a delegate; the delegates make up the legislative body of the AKC, voting on rules and electing directors. The American Kennel Club maintains the Stud Book, the record of every dog ever registered with the AKC, and publishes a variety of materials on purebred dogs, including a monthly magazine, books and numerous educational pamphlets. For more information, contact the AKC at the address listed in Chapter 9, "Resources."

of the area behind the withers and somewhat forward of the tail set), or if it is a roach back (convex or bulging curvature over the rear area of the topline).

The forelegs (front legs) are straight up and down. The hindquarters (rear assembly) have strong-muscled, slanting thighs (the upper thick part of the leg connected to the hip). They bend at the stifles (the "knee" joint between the thigh and the second thigh) and are straight from the hocks (the collection of bones forming the joint between the second thigh and the heel) to the heels (at the rear of the lowest part of the hind leg just above the foot). Hindquarters that are bowed (hocks turning away from each other) or cowhocked (hocks turning toward each other) are undesirable.

Gait

When moving at a trot, the Miniature Schnauzer's forelegs move straight forward. The hind legs move straight, traveling in the same planes as the forelegs. The feet point straight ahead. Faulted movements are single tracking (all footprints falling on a single line of travel), sidegaiting (dog moving forward with body at an angle), paddling in front (so named for its similarity to the swing and dip of a canoeist's paddle, the front legs swinging forward on a stiff outward arc) or high hackney knee action (the high lifting of the front feet resembling the gait of a hackney horse).

Coat

The show coat can make or break a dog's show career. It is double, with a hard, wiry outer coat and short undercoat. The head, neck and body coat must be plucked. When the stripped coat grows, it must be long enough for the judge to determine texture, while the coat length of neck, ears and skull is decidedly shorter. The furnishings (beard, eyebrows, legs and underbody hair) are fairly thick but not silky. The standard does not describe a clipped coat, because it is a disqualification in the ring, but it is highly attractive, practical and easily maintained.

It is the most popular and logical style for a Miniature Schnauzer pet.

Size

If a Miniature Schnauzer is under 12 inches or over 14 inches in height, the dog is disqualified. There is no need to disqualify, excuse or dismiss an over- or undersized pet Miniature Schnauzer from your home.

Color

There are three recognized colors, each being spectacularly beautiful: salt and pepper, black and silver and solid black. The colors and their

Miniature Schnauzers are not to be shown in a clipped coat; however, it is a highly attractive and practical cut for an everyday pet.

Three Miniature Schnauzer coat varieties pictured from left to right: salt and pepper, solid black, and black and silver.

Whether a show dog or a companion dog, your Miniature Schnauzer brings joy and love to her family and friends.

patterns are described in the standard and are easily understood.

ENJOYMENT OF YOUR DOG

No matter how closely or distantly the breed standard describes your Miniature Schnauzer, you'll clearly enjoy her. She'll adapt to whatever lifestyle you provide, at home or on vacation. She's a great camper, sailor or hiker, yet will lie contentedly at your feet on a cozy evening. She considers the guardianship of your home her mission in life and will demand the responsibility. Her insistent barking, however, is a cover-up for a soft heart: Don't be shocked if she leads an intruder to the family safe.

CHAPTER SEVEN

A Matter of Fact

L ike most breeds, the Miniature Schnauzer's precise development has been theorized by researchers, relying on artwork, descriptive references and records that survived the rigors of time. What is known is its membership in the three-sized schnauzer family: the Giant Schnauzer (25.5 to 27.5 inches for males, 23.5 to 25.5 inches for females); the Standard Schnauzer (18.5 to 19.5 inches for males, 17.5 to 18.5 inches for females); and the Miniature Schnauzer (12 to 14 inches for both sexes).

Each of the three sizes is a distinct and separate breed. The schnauzer family's origin in the cattle lands of Germany is undisputed.

This happy Miniature Schnauzer enjoys the comfort of his family's home, oblivious to his farm dog ancestry.

Translated into English from the German language, schnauzer means snout, muzzle, spout or nose.

A DROVER'S DOG

All authorities recognize the Standard Schnauzer as the original size and prototype of the three breeds. The common link connecting all theories of schnauzer ancestry concludes that stocky drovers' dogs formed the foundation from which the Rottweiler, Doberman Pinscher and Standard Schnauzer descended in the fifteenth century.

The crosses that produced the Standard Schnauzer are thought to be the black German Poodle and gray wolf Spitz upon wirehaired Pinscher stock. Bred for sagacity and fearlessness, he was an impressive rat catcher, yard dog and guard. In 1905, the first Standard Schnauzer was imported by a breeder in the United States.

While German drovers admired the Standard Schnauzer's appearance, soundness and power, they needed a larger specimen for cattle, so they generated the Giant Schnauzer—probably from early crosses with smooth-coated droving and dairymen's dogs. They then crossed the dogs with rough-haired sheepdogs and, eventually, with the black Great Dane and possibly with the Bouvier des Flandres.

DEVELOPMENT OF THE MINIATURE SCHNAUZER

Many authorities agree (and disagree) about how the breed or breeds crossed with the Standard Schnauzer to develop the Miniature, giving credit to the toy gray Spitz, Pomeranian, Poodle, Wire-haired Fox Terrier, Miniature Pinscher and Affenpinscher. The most widely accepted theory is that the

Affenpinscher and Poodle were crossed with small Standard Schnauzers to produce the Miniature Schnauzer. Whatever the crosses, aren't we fortunate that those founding German breeders admired the Standard Schnauzer but preferred it in a smaller package?

The Miniature, developed as a stable or farm dog, was used as a ratter and guard dog, though not a fighter. Because of his small size, he was invited to join the family as a companion, performing with great success. It was an unplanned function, highly appreciated and valued.

If your Miniature Schnauzer displays heightened pleasure chasing rabbits or squirrels, or adamantly stands his ground against an intrusion with a biteless bark, he is not being nonsensical; rather, he is yielding to his natural instincts as a ratter and guardian.

His primary function today is family pet, a mutually agreeable arrangement between owner and dog. While many Standards and Giants perform their usefully intended functions today, most have been liberated from their tasks, enjoying life as companions in the comfort of their owners' homes; some enjoy both roles simultaneously.

WHERE DID DOGS COME FROM?

It can be argued that dogs were right there at man's side from the beginning of time. As soon as human beings began to document their existence, the dog was among their drawings and inscriptions. Dogs were not just friends, they served a purpose: There were dogs to hunt birds, pull sleds, herd sheep, burrow after rats—even sit in laps! What your dog was originally bred to do influences the way he behaves. The American Kennel Club recognizes over 140 breeds, and there are hundreds more distinct breeds around the world. To make sense of the breeds, they are grouped according to their size or function. The AKC has seven groups:

1. Sporting
2. Working
3. Herding
4. Hounds
5. Terriers
6. Toys
7. Non Sporting

Can you name a breed from each group? Here's some help: (1) Golden Retriever, (2) Doberman Pinscher, (3) Collie, (4) Beagle, (5) Scottish Terrier, (6) Maltese, and (7) Dalmatian. All modern domestic dogs (*Canis familiaris*) are related, however different they look, and are all descended from *Canis lupus*, the gray wolf.

61

ESTABLISHMENT OF THE BREED

The Miniature Schnauzer is reported to have been established as long ago as 1859, and in 1889 Miniature Schnauzers were introduced as an exhibited breed at German shows. The earliest specimens bore little resemblance to the breed's appearance today.

Beyond his then stocky structure, terrierlike head, wiry coat and cropped ears, the prettification was absent. A ratter or guard didn't need stylized grooming, a richly colored coat, a profuse beard, eyebrows or leg furnishings. The early colors ranged from black, yellow and cream to black and tan. The occasional salt-and-pepper coat emerged later.

German breeders have developed an incredible number of breeds, and are admired for their patience and unfaltering efforts to fix type, for their documentation of breeding records and for their perseverance in tracing breed ancestries. Their expertise in developing the three sizes of schnauzers from various sources of crosses, producing each amazingly comparable to the others, is an extraordinary accomplishment. Among the ravages of World War II was the loss of early breeding records during the bombing of Germany. That is why there is an enormous void in the recorded history of breeds developed there.

THE EARLY IMPORTS

In 1923, two Miniature Schnauzers from the kennels of Rudolph Krappatch in Germany were imported by W. D. Goff of Massachusetts. Misfortune struck those imports. The male died, leaving no descendants, and the female's two litters were unproductive.

The Miniature Schnauzer was developed in Germany.

Although developed in 1859, the first Miniature Schnauzers did not arrive in America until the 1920s.

The following year, three females and one male from Krappatch's kennel were imported by Marie Slattery, whose kennel name was Marienhof. Three years later, Slattery imported a 3-year-old male. This dog, Cuno, is credited as having been more effectively influential on the breed's development in the United States than any other imported sire. Not a particularly outstanding specimen in every respect, Cuno nevertheless earned his American championship and passed on the few outstanding qualities he did display (and other qualities not evident) to his get (puppies), siring fourteen American champions, who produced the same fine qualities for many generations.

Intrigued by Slattery's early Miniature imports, other Americans imported 108 dogs and bitches during the following ten years, but extinction of most of those lines became common: Additional imports became unregistered pets or died without being registered.

CHANGED APPEARANCE

From time to time a breed's standard is changed. The Miniature Schnauzer's original maximum size was limited to 12 inches, and between 1930 and 1945, ear cropping was forbidden. Personal preferences to stylize the breed's

FAMOUS OWNERS OF THE MINIATURE SCHNAUZER

Errol Flynn
Tommy Lasorda
Robert and Elizabeth Dole

appearance led to the breeding of luscious furnishings and darkening the pepper coloration to create a sharper contrast in the salt-and-pepper coats. Those gains, however, softened the ideally hard texture of the coat, and a sleeker, terrier-type style of Miniature emerged in the late 1940s.

GAINING ADMIRERS

Interest in obedience greatly increased in 1946, introducing the breed to the general public. As the breed improved, Group placements and Best in Show wins increased, exposing the breed to show-minded individuals. Those exposures caused a proliferation of owners and breeders, and the popularity of Miniature Schnauzers rose in the 1960s.

Although the salt-and-pepper coat became and continues to be the most popular color, blacks and black and silvers began to gain favor

as the breed's popularity in general was soaring. Today, the quality of those formerly rare color-coated specimens is equal to the quality of the salt-and-pepper Miniatures, thanks to the breed's newer crop of pioneers, who appreciated and dedicated themselves to the rarity.

The breed's popularity is such that it is common to see at least one Miniature Schnauzer in most of the obedience classes in America. The breed is also popular with the viewing public: Miniature Schnauzers were a favorite breed in stage-performing dog acts in Germany.

The breed is also consistently pictured on boxes and bags of various dog foods and other canine-related products, and it is not uncommon to see a Miniature Schnauzer in non-dog television commercials and newspaper and magazine advertisements. The Miniature (usually clipped) appears as the starring family's or its neighbor's pet in movies or TV shows. There is little chance that such roles for these dogs will disappear, because let's face it: In a show coat, their appearance is outstanding; in a clipped coat, they're outstandingly cute.

With a face like this, it is no wonder why the Miniature Schnauzer is the fourteenth most popular breed in America.

Mr. Popularity

A conscientious breeder becomes nervous when his breed nears the number one spot in popularity, fearing the breed's downfall in the hands of less-than-knowledgeable opportunists anxious to breed quantity rather than quality of any popular breed. The Miniature Schnauzer's climb from obscurity was slow, but in the 1970s reached the top ten most popular breed status based on American Kennel Club registrations. It remained in the top ten for a number of years, just recently dipping lower.

In 1998, the Miniature Schnauzer had 31,063 individual registrations, ranking it the fourteenth most popular breed registered by the AKC. It is highly unlikely that the breed will ever be in danger of becoming unpopular: It is too appealing in appearance, temperament and intelligence. Add to that a vast network of dedicated, devoted and principled breeders who, as members of the parent club, are determined to protect the breed, and you have a breed loved by many and harmed by few.

CHAPTER EIGHT

On Good Behavior

by Ian Dunbar, Ph.D., MRCVS

Training is the jewel in the crown—the most important aspect of doggy husbandry. There is no more important variable

influencing dog behavior and temperament than the dog's education: A well-trained, well-behaved and good-natured puppydog is always a joy to live with, but an untrained and uncivilized dog can be a perpetual nightmare. Moreover, deny the dog an education and she will not have the opportunity to fulfill her own canine potential; neither will she have the ability to communicate effectively with her human companions.

Luckily, modern psychological training methods are easy, efficient, effective and, above all, considerably dog-friendly and user-friendly. Doggy education is as simple as it is enjoyable. But before you can have a good time play-training with your new dog, you have to learn what to do and how to do it. There is no bigger variable influencing the success of dog training than the owner's experience and expertise. Before you embark on the dog's education, you must first educate yourself.

BASIC TRAINING FOR OWNERS

Ideally, basic owner training should begin well before you select your dog. Find out all you can about your chosen breed first, then master rudimentary training and handling skills. If you already have your puppydog, owner training is a dire emergency—the clock is ticking! Especially for puppies, the first few weeks at home are the most important and influential days in the dog's life. Indeed, the cause of most adolescent and adult problems may be traced back to the initial days the pup explores her new home. This is the time to establish the status quo—to teach the puppydog how you would like her to behave and so prevent otherwise quite predictable problems.

In addition to consulting breeders and breed books such as this one (which understandably have a

This young owner is acclimating her new puppy to being on a lead.

positive breed bias), seek out as many pet owners with your breed as you can find. Good points are obvious. What you want to find out are the breed-specific problems, so you can nip them in the bud. In particular, you should talk to owners with adolescent dogs and make a list of all anticipated problems. Most important, test drive at least half a dozen adolescent and adult dogs of your breed yourself. An 8-week-old puppy is deceptively easy to handle, but she will acquire adult size, speed and strength in just four months, so you should learn now what to prepare for.

Puppy and pet dog training classes offer a convenient venue to locate pet owners and observe dogs

67

in action. For a list of suitable trainers in your area, contact the Association of Pet Dog Trainers (see Chapter 9). You may also begin your basic owner training by observing other owners in class. Watch as many classes and test drive as many dogs as possible. Select an upbeat, dog-friendly, people-friendly, fun-and-games, puppydog pet training class to learn the ropes. Also, watch training videos and read training books. You must find out what to do and how to do it before you have to do it.

PRINCIPLES OF TRAINING

Most people think training comprises teaching the dog to do things such as sit, speak and roll over, but even a 4-week-old pup knows how to do these things already. Instead, the first step in training involves teaching the dog human words for each dog behavior and activity and for each aspect of the dog's environment. That way you, the owner, can more easily participate in the dog's domestic education by directing her to perform specific actions appropriately, that is, at the right time, in the right place and so on. Training

opens communication channels, enabling an educated dog to at least understand her owner's requests.

In addition to teaching a dog what we want her to do, it is also necessary to teach her why she should do what we ask. Indeed, 95 percent of training revolves around motivating the dog to want to do what we want. Dogs often understand what their owners want; they just don't see the point of doing it—especially when the owner's repetitively boring and seemingly senseless instructions are totally at odds with much more pressing and exciting doggy distractions. It is not so much the dog that is being stubborn or dominant; rather, it is the owner who has failed to acknowledge the dog's needs and feelings and to approach training from the dog's point of view.

The Meaning of Instructions

The secret to successful training is learning how to use training lures to predict or prompt specific behaviors—to coax the dog to do what you want when you want. Any highly valued object (such as a treat or toy) may be used as a lure, which the dog will follow with her eyes and nose. Moving the lure in specific ways entices the dog to move her nose, head and entire body in specific ways. In fact, by learning the art of manipulating various lures, it is possible to teach the dog to assume virtually any body position and perform any action. Once you have control over the expression of the dog's behaviors and can elicit any body position or behavior at will, you can easily teach the dog to perform on request.

Tell your dog what you want her to do, use a lure to entice her to respond correctly, then profusely praise and maybe reward her once she performs the desired action. For example, verbally request "Fido, sit!"

while you move a squeaky toy upwards and backwards over the dog's muzzle (lure-movement and hand signal), smile knowingly as she looks up (to follow the lure) and sits down (as a result of canine anatomical engineering), then praise her to distraction ("Gooood Fido!"). Squeak the toy, offer a training treat and give your dog and yourself a pat on the back.

Being able to elicit desired responses over and over enables the owner to reward the dog over and over. Consequently, the dog begins to think training is fun. For example, the more the dog is rewarded for sitting, the more she enjoys sitting. Eventually the dog comes to realize that, whereas most sitting is

69

Miniature Schnauzers enjoy training, just like this good girl, who is retrieving a toy.

Rewarding your Miniature Schnauzer means a lot to her and teaches her that complying with your requests makes you happy and proud.

appreciated, sitting immediately upon request usually prompts especially enthusiastic praise and a slew of high-level rewards. The dog begins to sit on cue much of the time, showing that she is starting to grasp the meaning of the owner's verbal request and hand signal.

Why Comply?

Most dogs enjoy initial lure-reward training and are only too happy to comply with their owners' wishes. Unfortunately, repetitive drilling without appreciative feedback tends to diminish the dog's enthusiasm until she eventually fails to see the point of complying anymore. Moreover, as the dog approaches adolescence she becomes more easily distracted as she develops other interests. Lengthy sessions with repetitive exercises tend to bore and demotivate both parties. If it's not fun, the owner doesn't do it and neither does the dog.

Integrate training into your dog's life: The greater number of training sessions each day and the shorter they are, the more willingly compliant your dog will become. Make sure to have a short (just a few seconds) training interlude before every enjoyable canine activity. For example, ask your dog to sit to greet people, to sit before you throw her Frisbee and to sit for her supper. Really, sitting is no different from a canine "Please." Also, include numerous short training interludes during every enjoyable canine pastime, for example, when playing with the dog or when she is running in the park. In this fashion, doggy distractions may be effectively converted into rewards for training. Just as all games have rules, fun becomes training . . . and training becomes fun.

Eventually, rewards actually become unnecessary to continue motivating your dog. If trained with consideration and kindness, performing the desired behaviors will become self-rewarding and, in a sense, your dog will motivate herself. Just as it is not necessary to reward a human companion during an enjoyable walk in the park, or following a game of tennis, it is hardly necessary to reward our best friend—the dog—for walking by our side or while playing fetch. Human company during enjoyable activities is reward enough for most dogs.

Even though your dog has become self-motivating, it's still good to praise and pet her a lot and offer rewards once in a while, especially for a job well done. And if for no other reason, praising and rewarding others is good for the human heart.

TRAINER'S TOOLS

In addition to a willing dog, all you really need is a functional human brain, gentle hands, a loving heart and a good attitude. In terms of equipment, all dogs do require a quality buckle collar to sport dog tags and to attach the leash (for safety and to comply with local leash laws). Hollow chew toys (like Kongs or sterilized longbones) and a dog bed or collapsible crate are musts for housetraining. Three additional tools are required:

1. specific lures (training treats and toys) to predict and prompt specific desired behaviors;

2. rewards (praise, affection, training treats and toys) to reinforce for the dog what a lot of fun it all is; and

3. knowledge—how to convert the dog's favorite activities and games (potential distractions to training) into "life-rewards," which may be employed to facilitate training.

Giving a food reward isn't the only way to reward your pet. This Miniature Schnauzer gets her favorite toy after pleasing her owner.

The most powerful of these is knowledge. Education is the key! Watch training classes, participate in training classes, watch videos, read books, enjoy play-training with your dog and then your dog will say "Please," and your dog will say "Thank you!"

HOUSETRAINING

If dogs were left to their own devices, certainly they would chew, dig and bark for entertainment and then no doubt highlight a few areas of their living space with sprinkles of urine, in much the same way we decorate by hanging pictures. Consequently, when we ask a dog to live with us, we must teach her where she may dig, where she may perform her toilet duties, what she may chew and when she may bark. After all, when left at home alone for many hours, we cannot expect the dog to amuse herself by completing crosswords or watching the soaps on TV!

Also, it would be decidedly unfair to keep the house rules a secret from the dog, and then get angry and punish the poor critter for inevitably transgressing rules she did not even know existed. Remember:

Without adequate education and guidance, the dog will be forced to establish her own rules—doggy rules—and most probably will be at odds with the owner's view of domestic living.

Since most problems develop during the first few days the dog is at home, prospective dog owners must be certain they are quite clear about the principles of housetraining before they get a dog. Early misbehaviors quickly become established as the status quo—becoming firmly entrenched as hard-to-break bad habits, which set the precedent for years to come. Make sure to teach your dog good habits right from the start. Good habits are just as hard to break as bad ones!

Ideally, when a new dog comes home, try to arrange for someone to be present as much as possible during the first few days (for adult dogs) or weeks for puppies. With only a little forethought, it is surprisingly easy to find a puppy sitter, such as a retired person, who would be willing to eat from your refrigerator and watch your television while keeping an eye on the newcomer to encourage the dog to play with chew toys and to ensure she goes outside on a regular basis.

Potty Training

To teach the dog where to relieve herself:

1. never let her make a single mistake;

2. let her know where you want her to go; and

3. handsomely reward her for doing so: "GOOOOOOOD DOG!!!" liver treat, liver treat, liver treat!

Preventing Mistakes

A single mistake is a training disaster, since it heralds many more in future weeks. And each time the dog soils the house, this further reinforces the dog's unfortunate preference for an indoor, carpeted toilet. Do not let an unhousetrained dog have full run of the house.

When you are away from home, or cannot pay full attention, confine the dog to an area where elimination is appropriate, such as an outdoor run or, better still, a small, comfortable indoor kennel with access to an outdoor run. When confined in this manner, most dogs will naturally housetrain themselves.

If that's not possible, confine the dog to an area, such as a utility

HOUSETRAINING 1-2-3

1. Prevent Mistakes. When you can't supervise your puppy, confine her in a single room or in her crate (but don't leave her for too long!). Puppy-proof the area by laying down newspapers so that if she does make a mistake, it won't matter.

2. Teach Where. Take your puppy to the spot you want her to use every hour.

3. When she goes, praise her profusely and give her three favorite treats.

room, kitchen, basement or garage, where elimination may not be desired in the long run but as an interim measure it is certainly preferable to doing it all around the house. Use newspaper to cover the floor of the dog's day room. The newspaper may be used to soak up the urine and to wrap up and dispose of the feces. Once your dog develops a preferred spot for eliminating, it is only necessary to cover that part of the floor with newspaper. The smaller papered area may then be moved (only a little each day) towards the door to the outside. Thus the dog will develop the tendency to go to the door when she needs to relieve herself.

73

Never confine an unhousetrained dog to a crate for long periods. Doing so would force the dog to soil the crate and ruin its usefulness as an aid for housetraining (see the following discussion).

Teaching Where

In order to teach your dog where you would like her to do her business, you have to be there to direct the proceedings—an obvious, yet often neglected, fact of life. In order to be there to teach the dog where to go, you need to know when she needs to go. Indeed, the success of housetraining depends on the owner's ability to predict these times. Certainly, a regular feeding schedule will facilitate prediction somewhat, but there is nothing like "loading the deck" and influencing the timing of the outcome yourself!

Whenever you are at home, make sure the dog is under constant supervision and/or confined to a small area. If already well trained, simply instruct the dog to lie down in her bed or basket. Alternatively, confine the dog to a crate (doggy den) or tie-down (a short, 18-inch lead that can be clipped to an eye hook in the baseboard near her bed). Short-term close confinement strongly inhibits urination and

This Miniature Schnauzer loves to sail through the tire jump.

defecation, since the dog does not want to soil her sleeping area. Thus, when you release the puppydog each hour, she will definitely need to urinate immediately and defecate every third or fourth hour. Keep the dog confined to her doggy den and take her to her intended toilet area each hour, every hour and on the hour. When taking your dog outside, instruct her to sit quietly before opening the door—she will soon learn to sit by the door when she needs to go out!

Teaching Why

Being able to predict when the dog needs to go enables the owner to be on the spot to praise and reward the dog. Each hour, hurry the dog to the intended toilet area in the yard, issue the appropriate instruction ("Go pee!" or "Go poop!"), then give the dog three to four minutes to produce. Praise and offer a couple of training treats when successful. The treats are important because many people fail to praise their dogs with feeling . . . and housetraining is hardly the time for understatement. So either loosen up and enthusiastically praise that dog: "Wuzzerwuzzer-wuzzer, hoooser good wuffer

OWNING A PARTY ANIMAL

It's a fact: The more of the world your puppy is exposed to, the more comfortable she'll be in it. Once your puppy's had her shots, start taking her everywhere with you. Encourage friendly interaction with strangers, expose her to different environments (towns, fields, beaches) and most important, enroll her in a puppy class where she'll get to play with other puppies. These simple, fun, shared activities will develop your pup into a confident socialite; reliable around other people and dogs.

den? Hoooo went pee for Daddy?" Or say "Good dog!" as best you can and offer the treats for effect.

Following elimination is an ideal time for a spot of play-training in the yard or house. Also, an empty dog may be allowed greater freedom around the house for the next half hour or so, just as long as you keep an eye out to make sure she does not get into other kinds of mischief. If you are preoccupied and cannot pay full attention, confine the dog to her doggy den once more to enjoy a peaceful snooze or to play with her many chew toys.

If your dog does not eliminate within the allotted time outside— no biggie! Back to her doggy den,

A supervised or confined dog has less chance to err in his house-training.

and then try again after another hour.

As I own large dogs, I always feel more relaxed walking an empty dog, knowing that I will not need to finish our stroll weighted down with bags of feces!

Beware of falling into the trap of walking the dog to get her to eliminate. The good ol' dog walk is such an enormous highlight in the dog's life that it represents the single biggest potential reward in domestic dogdom. However, when in a hurry, or during inclement weather, many owners abruptly terminate the walk the moment the dog has done her business. This, in effect, severely

punishes the dog for doing the right thing, in the right place at the right time. Consequently, many dogs become strongly inhibited from eliminating outdoors because they know it will signal an abrupt end to an otherwise thoroughly enjoyable walk.

Instead, instruct the dog to relieve herself in the yard prior to going for a walk. If you follow the above instructions, most dogs soon learn to eliminate on cue. As soon as the dog eliminates, praise (and offer a treat or two)—"Good dog! Let's go walkies!" Use the walk as a reward for eliminating in the yard. If the dog does not go, put her back in her doggy den and think about a walk later on. You will find with a "No feces—no walk" policy, your dog will become one of the fastest defecators in the business.

If you do not have a backyard, instruct the dog to eliminate right outside your front door prior to the walk. Not only will this facilitate clean up and disposal of the feces in your own trash can but, also, the walk may again be used as a colossal reward.

CHEWING AND BARKING

Short-term close confinement also teaches the dog that occasional quiet moments are a reality of domestic living.

When confining the dog, make sure she always has an impressive array of suitable chew toys. Kongs and sterilized longbones (both readily available from pet stores) make the best chew toys, since they are hollow and may be stuffed with treats to heighten the dog's interest.

If stuffed chew toys are reserved especially for times the dog is confined, the puppydog will soon learn to enjoy quiet moments in her doggy den and she will quickly develop a chew-toy habit a good habit! This is a simple autoshaping process; all the owner has to do is

So many toys, so little time!

Toys that Earn Their Keep

To entertain even the most distracted of dogs, while you're home or away, have a selection of the following toys on hand: hollow chew toys (like Kongs, sterilized hollow longbones and cubes or balls that can be stuffed with kibble). Smear peanut butter or honey on the inside of the hollow toy or bone, stuff the bone with kibble and your dog will think of nothing else but working the object to get at the food. Great to take your dog's mind off the fact that you've left the house.

set up the situation and the dog all but trains herself—easy and effective. Even when the dog is given run of the house, her first inclination will be to indulge her rewarding chew-toy habit rather than destroy less-attractive household articles. Similarly, a chew-toy chewer will be less inclined to scratch and chew herself excessively. Also, if the dog busies herself as a recreational chewer, she will be less inclined to develop into a recreational barker or digger when left at home alone.

Stuff a number of chew toys whenever the dog is left confined and remove the extra-special-tasting treats when you return. Your dog will now amuse herself with her chew toys before falling asleep and then resume playing with her chew toys when she expects you to return. Since most owner-absent misbehavior occurs right after you leave and right before your expected return, your puppydog will now be conveniently preoccupied with her chew toys at these times.

Sit, Down, Stand and Rollover

Teaching the dog a variety of body positions is easy for owner and dog, impressive for spectators and extremely useful for all. Using lure-reward techniques, it is possible to train several positions at once to verbal commands or hand signals (which impress the socks off onlookers).

Sit and down—the two control commands—prevent or resolve nearly a hundred behavior problems. For example, if the dog happily and obediently sits or lies down when requested, she cannot jump on visitors, dash out the front door, run around and chase her tail, pester other dogs, harass cats or annoy family, friends or strangers. "Sit" or "Down" are the best emergency commands for off-leash control.

It is easier to teach and maintain a reliable sit than maintain a reliable recall. Sit is the purest and simplest of commands—either the dog is sitting or she is not. If there is any change of circumstances or potential danger in the park, for example, simply instruct the dog to sit. If she sits, you have a number of options: Allow the dog to resume playing when she is safe, walk up and put the dog on leash or call the dog. The dog will be much more likely to come when called if she has already acknowledged her compliance by sitting. If the dog does not sit in the park—train her to!

Stand and rollover-stay are the two positions for examining the dog.

Your veterinarian will love you to distraction if you take a little time to teach the dog to stand still and roll over and play possum. Also, your vet bills will be smaller because it will take the veterinarian less time to examine your dog. The rollover-stay is an especially useful command and is really just a variation of the down-stay: Whereas the dog lies prone in the traditional down, she lies supine in the rollover-stay.

As with teaching come and sit, the training techniques to teach the dog to assume all other body positions on cue are user-friendly and dog-friendly. Simply give the appropriate request, lure the dog into the desired body position using a

This Miniature Schnauzer performs a "Down" command for a food lure.

training treat or toy and then praise (and maybe reward) the dog as soon as she complies. Try not to touch the dog to get her to respond. If you teach the dog by guiding her into position, the dog will quickly learn that rump-pressure means sit, for example, but as yet you still have no control over your dog if she is just 6 feet away. It will still be necessary to teach the dog to sit on request. So do not make training a time-consuming two-step process; instead, teach the dog to sit to a verbal request or hand signal from the outset. Once the dog sits willingly

An example of a "Down" command.

when requested, by all means use your hands to pet the dog when she does so.

To teach down when the dog is already sitting, say "Fido, down!," hold the lure in one hand (palm down) and lower that hand to the floor between the dog's forepaws. As the dog lowers her head to follow the lure, slowly move the lure away from the dog just a fraction (in front of her paws). The dog will lie down as she stretches her nose forward to follow the lure. Praise the dog when she does so. If the dog stands up, you pulled the lure away too far and too quickly.

When teaching the dog to lie down from the standing position, say "Down" and lower the lure to the floor as before. Once the dog has lowered her forequarters and assumed a play bow, gently and slowly move the lure towards the dog between her forelegs. Praise the dog as soon as her rear end plops down.

After just a couple of trials it will be possible to alternate sits and downs and have the dog energetically perform doggy push-ups. Praise the dog a lot, and after half a dozen or so push-ups reward the dog with a training treat or toy. You will notice the more energetically you move your arm—upwards (palm up) to get the dog to sit, and downwards (palm down) to get the dog to lie down—the more energetically the dog responds to your requests. Now try training the dog in silence and you will notice she has also learned to respond to hand signals. Yeah! Not too shabby for the first session.

To teach stand from the sitting position, say "Fido, stand," slowly move the lure half a dog-length away from the dog's nose, keeping it at nose level, and praise the dog as she stands to follow the lure. As soon as the dog stands, lower the lure to just beneath the dog's chin to entice her to look down; otherwise she will stand and then sit immediately. To prompt the dog to stand from the down position, move the lure half a dog-length upwards and away from the dog, holding the lure at standing nose height from the floor.

Teaching rollover is best started from the down position, with the dog lying on one side, or at least with both hind legs stretched out on the same side. Say "Fido, bang!" and move the lure backwards and alongside the dog's muzzle to her elbow (on the side of her outstretched hind

FINDING A TRAINER

Have fun with your dog, take a training class! But don't just sign on any dotted line, find a trainer whose approach and style you like and whose students (and their dogs) are really learning. Ask to visit a class to observe a trainer in action. For the names of trainers near you, ask your veterinarian, your pet supply store, your dog owning neighbors or call (800) PET DOGS (the Association of Pet Dog Trainers).

legs). Once the dog looks to the side and backwards, very slowly move the lure upwards to the dog's shoulder and backbone. Tickling the dog in the goolies (groin area) often invokes a reflex-raising of the hind leg as an appeasement gesture, which facilitates the tendency to roll over. If you move the lure too quickly and the dog jumps into the standing position, have patience and start again. As soon as the dog rolls onto her back, keep the lure stationary and mesmerize the dog with a relaxing tummy rub.

To teach rollover-stay when the dog is standing or moving, say "Fido, bang!" and give the appropriate hand signal (with index finger pointed and thumb cocked in true Sam Spade fashion), then in one fluid movement lure her to first lie down and then rollover-stay as above.

Teaching the dog to stay in each of the above four positions becomes a piece of cake after first teaching the dog not to worry at the toy or treat training lure. This is best accomplished by hand feeding dinner kibble. Hold a piece of kibble firmly in your hand and softly instruct "Off!" Ignore any licking and slobbering for however long the dog worries at the treat, but say "Take it!" and offer the kibble the instant the dog breaks contact with her muzzle. Repeat this a few times, and then up the ante and insist the dog remove her muzzle for one whole second before offering the kibble. Then progressively refine your criteria and have the dog not touch your hand (or treat) for longer and longer periods on each trial, such as for two seconds, four seconds, then six, ten, fifteen, twenty, thirty seconds and so on.

The dog soon learns: (1) worrying at the treat never gets results, whereas (2) noncontact is often rewarded after a variable time lapse.

Teaching "Off!" has many useful applications in its own right. Additionally, instructing the dog not

82

to touch a training lure often produces spontaneous and magical sit or down stays. To request the dog to stand-stay, for example, and not to touch the lure, at first set your sights on a short two-second stay before rewarding the dog. (Remember, every long journey begins with a single step.) However, on subsequent trials, gradually and progressively increase the length of stay required to receive a reward. In no time at all your dog will stand calmly for a minute or so.

RELEVANCY TRAINING

Once you have taught the dog what you expect her to do when requested to come, sit, lie down, stand, rollover and stay, the time is right to teach the dog why she should comply with your wishes. The secret is to have many (many) extremely short training interludes (two to five seconds each) at numerous (numerous) times during the course of the dog's day. Especially work with the dog immediately before the dog's good times and during the dog's good times. For example, ask your dog to sit and/or lie down each time before opening doors, serving meals, offering treats and tummy rubs; ask the dog to perform a few controlled doggy push-ups before letting her off leash or throwing a tennis ball; and perhaps request the dog to sit-down-sit-stand-down-stand-rollover before inviting her to cuddle on the couch.

Similarly, request the dog to sit many times during play or on walks, and in no time at all the dog will be only too pleased to follow your instructions because she has learned that a compliant response heralds all sorts of goodies. Basically all you are trying to teach the dog is how to say please: "Please throw the tennis ball. Please may I snuggle on the couch."

Remember, it is important to keep training interludes short and to have many short sessions each and every day. The shortest (and most useful) session comprises asking the dog to sit and then go play during a play session. When trained this way, your dog will soon associate training with good times. In fact, the dog may be unable to distinguish between training and good times and, indeed, there should be no distinction. The warped concept that training involves forcing the dog to comply and/or dominating her will is totally at odds with the picture of a truly well-trained dog. In reality, enjoying a game of training with a dog is no different from enjoying a game of backgammon or tennis with a friend; and walking with a dog should be no different from strolling with a spouse or with buddies on the golf course.

WALK BY YOUR SIDE

Many people attempt to teach a dog to heel by putting her on a leash and physically correcting the dog when she makes mistakes. There are a number of things seriously wrong with this approach, the first being that most people do not want

A dog and owner enjoy a leisurely walk— side by side.

precision heeling; rather, they simply want the dog to follow or walk by their side. Second, when physically restrained during "training," even though the dog may grudgingly mope by your side when "hand-cuffed" on leash, let's see what happens when she is off leash. History! The dog is in the next county because she never enjoyed walking with you on leash and you have no control over her off leash. So let's just teach the dog off leash from the outset to want to walk with us. Third, if the dog has not been trained to heel, it is a trifle hasty to think about punishing the poor dog for making mistakes and breaking heeling rules she didn't even know existed. This is simply not fair!

It is a good idea to practice with your dog on lead in the house.

Surely, if the dog had been adequately taught how to heel, she would seldom make mistakes and hence there would be no need to correct the dog. Remember, each mistake and each correction (punishment) advertise the trainer's inadequacy, not the dog's. The dog is not stubborn, she is not stupid and she is not bad. Even if she were, she would still require training, so let's train her properly.

Let's teach the dog to enjoy following us and to want to walk by our side off leash. Then it will be easier to teach high-precision off-leash heeling patterns if desired. Before going on outdoor walks, it is necessary to teach the dog not to pull. Then it becomes easy to teach on-leash walking and heeling because the dog already wants to walk with you, she is familiar with the desired walking and heeling positions and she knows not to pull.

FOLLOWING

Start by training your dog to follow you. Many puppies will follow if you simply walk away from them and maybe click your fingers or chuckle. Adult dogs may require additional enticement to stimulate them to follow, such as a training lure or, at the very least, a lively trainer. To teach the dog to follow: (1) keep walking and (2) walk away from the dog. If the dog attempts to lead or lag, change pace; slow down if the dog forges too far ahead, but speed up if she lags too far behind. Say "Steady!" or "Easy!" each time before you slow down and "Quickly!" or "Hustle!" each time before you speed up, and the dog will learn to change pace on cue. If the dog lags or leads too far, or if she wanders right or left, simply walk quickly in the opposite direction and maybe even run away from the dog and hide.

CHAPTER NINE

Resources

BOOKS

About Miniature Schnauzers

Janish, Anton. *Guide to Owning a Miniature Schnauzer.* Neptune, NJ: Tfh Publications, 1996.

Kiedrowski, Dan. *The New Miniature Schnauzer.* New York: Howell Book House, 1997.

Newman, Peter. *Miniature Schnauzers Today.* New York: Howell Book House, 1998.

Rugh, Karla S. *Miniature Schnauzers: A Complete Pet Owner's Manual.* Hauppauge: Barrons, 1997.

About Health Care

American Kennel Club. *American Kennel Club Dog Care and Training.* New York: Howell Book House, 1991.

Carlson, Delbert, DVM, and James Giffen, MD. *Dog Owner's Home Veterinary Handbook.* New York: Howell Book House, 1992.

DeBitetto, James, DVM, and Sarah Hodgson. *You & Your Puppy.* New York: Howell Book House, 1995.

Lane, Marion. *The Humane Society of the United States Complete Guide to Dog Care.* New York: Little, Brown & Co., 1998.

McGinnis, Terri. *The Well Dog Book.* New York: Random House, 1991.

Schwartz, Stephanie, DVM. *First Aid for Dogs: An Owner's Guide to a Happy Healthy Pet.* New York: Howell Book House, 1998.

Volhard, Wendy and Kerry L. Brown. *The Holistic Guide for a Healthy Dog.* New York: Howell Book House, 1995.

About Training

Ammen, Amy. *Training in No Time.* New York: Howell Book House, 1995.

Benjamin, Carol Lea. *Mother Knows Best.* New York: Howell Book House, 1985.

Bohnenkamp, Gwen. *Manners for the Modern Dog*. San Francisco: Perfect Paws, 1990.

Dunbar, Ian, Ph.D., MRCVS. *Dr. Dunbar's Good Little Book*. James & Kenneth Publishers, 2140 Shattuck Ave. #2406, Berkeley, CA 94704. (510) 658-8588. Order from Publisher.

Evans, Job Michael. *People, Pooches and Problems*. New York: Howell Book House, 1991.

Palika, Liz. *All Dogs Need Some Training*. New York: Howell Book House, 1997.

Volhard, Jack and Melissa Bartlett. *What All Good Dogs Should Know: The Sensible Way to Train*. New York: Howell Book House, 1991.

About Activities

Hall, Lynn. *Dog Showing for Beginners*. New York: Howell Book House, 1994.

O'Neil, Jackie. *All About Agility*. New York: Howell Book House, 1998.

Simmons-Moake, Jane. *Agility Training, The Fun Sport for All Dogs*. New York: Howell Book House, 1991.

Vanacore, Connie. *Dog Showing: An Owner's Guide*. New York: Howell Book House, 1990.

Volhard, Jack and Wendy. *The Canine Good Citizen*. New York: Howell Book House, 1994.

MAGAZINES

The AKC GAZETTE, The Official Journal for the Sport of Purebred Dogs
American Kennel Club
260 Madison Ave.
New York, NY 10016
www.akc.org

Dog Fancy
Fancy Publications
3 Burroughs
Irvine, CA 92618
(714) 855-8822
http://dogfancy.com

Dog World
Maclean Hunter Publishing Corp.
500 N. Dearborn, Ste. 1100
Chicago, IL 60610
(312) 396-0600
www.dogworldmag.com

PetLife: Your Companion Animal Magazine
Magnolia Media Group
1400 Two Tandy Center
Fort Worth, TX 76102
(800) 767-9377
www.petlifeweb.com

Dog & Kennel
7-L Dundas Circle
Greensboro, NC 27407
(336) 292-4047
www.dogandkennel.com

More Information About Miniature Schnauzers

National Breed Club

AMERICAN MINIATURE
SCHNAUZER CLUB
Corresponding Secretary:
    Carma Ewer
    8882 South Easthills Drive
    Sandy, UT 84093-1813
    AMSCsec@aol.com

Breeder Contact:
    Amy Gordon
    802 Upland Road
    West Palm Beach, FL 34014
    (561) 366-1038
    aragonms@worldnet.att.net

Breed Rescue:
    Bolivia Powell
    (214) 363-5630

The Club can send you information on
all aspects of the breed including the
names and addresses of breed clubs in
your area, as well as obedience clubs.
Inquire about membership.

The American Kennel Club

The American Kennel Club (AKC),
devoted to the advancement of purebred
dogs, is the oldest and largest registry
organization in this country. Every breed
recognized by the AKC has a national
(parent) club. National clubs are a great
source of information on your breed.

The affiliated clubs hold AKC events
and use AKC rules to hold performance
events, dog shows, educational programs, health clinics and training classes. The AKC staff is divided between
offices in New York City and Raleigh,
North Carolina. The AKC has an excellent Web site that provides information
on the organization and all AKC-
recognized breeds. The address is
www.akc.org.

For registration and performance
events information, or for customer ser-
vice, contact:

THE AMERICAN KENNEL CLUB
5580 Centerview Dr., Suite 200
Raleigh, NC 27606
(919) 233-9767

The AKC's executive offices and the
AKC Library (open to the public) are at
this address:

THE AMERICAN KENNEL CLUB
260 Madison Ave.
New York, NY 10016
(212) 696-8200 (general information)
(212) 696-8246 (AKC Library)
www.akc.org

UNITED KENNEL CLUB
100 E. Kilgore Rd.
Kalamazoo, MI 49001-5598
(616) 343-9020
www.ukcdogs.com

AMERICAN RARE BREED
ASSOCIATION
9921 Frank Tippett Rd.
Cheltenham, MD 20623
(301) 868-5718 (voice or fax)
www.arba.org

CANADIAN KENNEL CLUB
89 Skyway Ave., Ste. 100
Etobicoke, Ontario
Canada M9W 6R4
(416) 675-5511
www.ckc.ca

ORTHOPEDIC FOUNDATION
FOR ANIMALS (OFA)
2300 E. Nifong Blvd.
Columbia, MO 65201-3856
(314) 442-0418
www.offa.org/

Trainers

Animal Behavior & Training Associates
(ABTA)
9018 Balboa Blvd., Ste. 591
Northridge, CA 91325
(800) 795-3294
www.Good-dawg.com

Association of Pet Dog Trainers
(APDT)
(800) PET-DOGS
www.apdt.com

National Association of Dog
Obedience Instructors (NADOI)
729 Grapevine Highway, Ste. 369
Hurst, TX 76054-2085
www.kimberly.uidaho.edu/nadoi

Associations

Delta Society
P.O. Box 1080
Renton, WA 98507-1080
(Promotes the human/animal bond
through pet-assisted therapy and other
programs)
www.petsforum.com/
DELTASOCIETY/dsi400.htm

Dog Writers Association of America
(DWAA)
Sally Cooper, Secretary
222 Woodchuck Lane
Harwinton, CT 06791
www.dwaa.org

National Association for Search and
Rescue (NASAR)
4500 Southgate Place, Ste. 100
Chantilly, VA 20157
(703) 222-6277
www.nasar.org

Therapy Dogs International
6 Hilltop Rd.
Mendham, NJ 07945

89

OTHER USEFUL RESOURCES— WEB SITES

General Information— Links to Additional Sites, On-Line Shopping

www.k9web.com – resources for the dog
world

www.netpet.com – pet related products,
software and services

www.apapets.com – The American Pet
Association

www.dogandcatbooks.com – book
catalog

www.dogbooks.com – on-line bookshop

www.animal.discovery.com/ – cable
television channel on-line

Health

www.avma.org – American Veterinary Medical Association (AVMA).

www.aplb.org – Association for Pet Loss Bereavement (APLB)—contains an index of national hot lines for on-line and office counseling.

www.netfopets.com/AskTheExperts.html – veterinary questions answered on-line.

Breed Information

www.bestdogs.com/news/ – newsgroup

www.cheta.net/connect/canine/breeds/ – Canine Connections Breed Information Index